WAYS OF PRAYER SERIES

Basil Pennington, OCSO
Consulting Editor

Volume 11

God's Time is the Best Time

by

Anselm Hufstader

Michael Glazier, Inc.
Wilmington, Delaware

ABOUT THE AUTHOR

Anselm Hufstader is a Benedictine monk of Portsmouth Abbey in Rhode Island. He studied theology at the Benedictine College of Sant' Anselmo in Rome, where he was ordained in 1967. Since 1968 he has been on the faculty of the Portsmouth Abbey School, and was appointed its headmaster in 1973. This is his first book.

Published in 1984 by: MICHAEL GLAZIER, INC., 1723 Delaware Avenue, Wilmington, Delaware 19806 and Dominican Publications, St. Saviour's, Dublin, Ireland.

Library of Congress Catalog Card Number: 83-83254
International Standard Book Number:
   Ways of Prayer series: 0-89453-282-0
   GOD'S TIME
      Paperback: 0-89453-385-1 (Michael Glazier, Inc.)
      Cloth: 0-89453-386-X (Michael Glazier, Inc.)
      Paperback: 0-907271-27-8 (Dominican Publications)

Cover design by Lillian Brulc

Typography by Susan H. Pickett

Printed in the United States of America

CONTENTS

A Year of Grace

The Spirit of the Lord God is upon me,
    because the Lord has anointed me
to bring good tidings to the afflicted;
    he has sent me to bind the brokenhearted,
to proclaim liberty to the captives,
    and the opening of the prison to those who are bound;
to proclaim the year of the Lord's favor . . . (Is. 61:1-2)

1979. There was no one event that made that year special. I am not even sure when it began or ended; perhaps it has not ended yet. I only know that there has been a time of grace, of the Lord's favor. On the outside, my life seems the same as it was last year and the year before. These might also have been years of grace. Grace is given to us inwardly, and we often fail to recognize it. Only now and then do we sense something, a new design in our lives or a new quality of being. We want to share it in speech, but what language can we use to describe what we ourselves only see dimly? We search for words, trying to teach ourselves.

As I reflect on my own past, I see that my chronology, the list of major events in my life, does little to help me understand myself. I began something, I ended something else, someone died, I went on a journey, I returned. *Curriculum vitae*, the running-out of my life. Has this sequence a meaning, a discernible shape? Caught in the middle of it, I cannot tell. What I do see in my life, as you do in yours, is repetition. Change as we may, basic actions, feelings, struggles and resolutions come around again and again. We started to trace our story, and found we were telling the turns of a wheel. Our life-cycles can be graphed, and our positions on it plotted. Then there are wheels within wheels, the epi-cycles of medical, financial, nutritional, or psychological patterns. The Ptolemaic astronomers of the body's constellations offer to diagram us, and tell us if we are going to have a good day. Are we moving forward (and if so, to what goal?) or just in circles?

I think about myself the way I do because I am a teacher and because I am a monk. I attempt to start young people reflecting on their own experience, thinking responsibly for themselves. Teaching religion, and a great deal of personal interaction with students, have forced me to carry on that same reflection for myself. As a monk, I take part in a daily life of prayer, communal and private, in the framework of the Church's liturgy. Whether I am singing our daily office or giving a Sunday homily, the themes of the liturgical year are a constant preoccupation. I am not always as conscious of them as I am of the issues and problems I encounter in my teaching, but they are always present, as harmony is to a song.

Teaching and liturgy: two elements in reflection about my experience.

I looked for a unique story in my life and found repetition, a set of cycles. The liturgical year is also a cycle, although an unusual one. Its most important annual feasts commemorate specific events in the past, things that happened once and for all. There are many Christmases, but there was one Incarnation. Each year we celebrate Easter because only one man rose from the dead. Time after time we remember things which cannot be repeated. Thinking about myself, I looked for uniqueness and found repetition. Thinking about the liturgy, I began with repetition and was led to the uniqueness of sacred events. Thinking about my own chronology helps me to understand myself less than does meditation on the Church year, the year of grace.

No matter how much we try to modernize it, the ‚liturgy remains of its nature a primitive thing. It is made up of seasons and, like them, represents the earliest concerns of man. In winter the year ends and the sun falls to increasing darkness. Then it revives, and there is a new year. First the feast of lights, *sol invictus*, but now the morning star of Christ, an unrepeatable event. The ground is frozen, a grave for seeds to die in, but then life springs up. It is the new moon, the time of beginnings. It is the struggle of Marduk and Tiamat, order and chaos. It is the escape from Pharaoh, the passover through the chaotic waters of death, and now the once-and-for-all triumph of Jesus over his grave. Mankind was centuries in preparing for these mysteries, but today's culture has quickly forgotten them. Urban living and its technology have brought a new set of rhythms, a new sensibility. We have lost touch with the ancient mysteries, and therefore with ourselves. The conflicts of light and darkness, the sequence of love and birth, the miracle of fresh beginnings and the longing for imminent happiness — all these lie deep in our personalities, often forgotten. Our new calendar of civic and sentimental holidays is a poor copy of what we have lost. Jung speaks of the secular atheist, living prosperously in the city, who scoffs at the idea of Resurrection, and would no more go to church at Easter than on any other day. The miracle of new life, rising up out of the ground, means nothing to him. And yet, what is he doing on the morning of Easter? He is in his garden, with his children, looking for eggs. Has it even occurred to him to wonder why he is carrying out this strange ritual? What is its significance? If you ask him, he will say, "Oh, it is just something we've always done."[1]

Living in secular time, we live in ignorance of ourselves. The Christian year redeems the time. We celebrate it, and receive ourselves back. I begin with my secular disappointment, when I looked for myself as unique and found myself as part of *karma*, repetition of worldly cycles. Some religions teach liberation from *karma*, but Christianity accepts it as fact and redeems it. Even the humblest repetitions — sleeping and waking, eating and drinking, sadness and joy — are made noble in the rhythm of celebration. Yet this is not man's work, although man contributes his symbols and dramatic sense. Barzini says of the Italians that they make of life a drama, a Baroque spectacle, in order to render dignified and acceptable the hard facts of poverty, suffering and death.[2] Doubtless we do this, but it is not our efforts which give meaning to our liturgy. Those who have thought otherwise, and have bent

[1]"Archaic Man," *Civilization in Transition: The Collected Works of C. G. Jung*, 10 (New York: Bollingen, 1964), p. 72.

[2]Luigi Barzini, *The Italians* (New York: Atheneum, 1964), pp. 325-339.

liturgy to the service of man, have had to endure the pain of watching their efforts become irrelevant, then obsolete. The reason why Christianity redeems our time is because the primal, repeated events of birth and death are subsumed into the one, unique birth and death of the Lord. This uniqueness, at the end of repetition, gives my uniqueness back to me. In the world, I am caught up in the wheels of humanity. Here, before the redeeming acts of Christ, I rediscover myself as a person of special significance.

The chapters that follow were not designed as reflections on the liturgical year. I had set myself the task of reflecting on my recent past, my year of grace, in order to take stock of the present and future. It was shortly after I began this that self-understanding — to the extent that I gained it — suggested itself in terms of the Christian year. My language is that of human concerns, and what I discovered was that this is precisely the language of the great liturgical seasons. I did not begin with Advent. I began with desire, and this led to Advent, and that led to a better understanding of desire.

Then there was a second discovery. My experience of grace seemed to take a shape, a pattern, which also appears to me in the sequence of liturgical seasons. It is a threefold sequence which begins with some human initiative, an assertion of the self before the divine. I express desire for God, or the need for forgiveness. Then there is an action of God, a response to this initiative. (Some theologians will want to say that my initiative was itself an action of God — let it be so; here I speak only of my experience.) This action of God surprises me. It is not what I expected, and I am even disappointed until I realize that God's way of acting goes beyond my furthest expectations. Naaman wanted to be cured by an impressive miracle, and all he got was a bath in a dirty river. He also got perfect healing. We are humbled by the greatness of God's gifts. If this second stage, where God acts, takes away our initiative, the third stage restores it to us. Here God himself shows us his glory and gives us understanding. He raises us up and sends us out. We began by seeking ourselves, and now our true identity is given us by God. The essence of this sequence is that the ego, the self as center, is displaced by the Other — first God, then neighbor. I experience this displacement of the self as the mystery of salvation. It is a miracle which happens in an endless variety of ways, and keeps happening again and again as the ego struggles to return to the center. Some of the ways it has happened to me — that is my theme.

The liturgical sequence of miracles occurs in two cycles. First there is Advent, Nativity, and Epiphany. Man's desire ascends. God descends in a humble birth. There is meeting between man and God, and salvation begins. This is the cycle of desire and knowledge. Then there is Lent, Resurrection, and Pentecost. Man experiences guilt and seeks forgiveness. God, in dying, penetrates to the depth of that guilt and in rising overcomes it. God and man meet again in the Spirit, man finds a purpose, and salvation begins for others. This is the cycle of death and life. First my desires and needs. Then the unexpected deed of God. Finally true fulfillment of desire, true being and life, but with the center displaced.

The second stage is the key to the others, but it eludes me. How can I understand these acts of grace which change selfish desire for love into the ability to prefer others to myself? Ambition for success into consecration to service? Flashy intelligence into truly sensitive understanding? The noise of shallow bravado into the quiet of supernatural courage? Intolerance of slight faults into patience under great burdens? "He has put down the mighty from their seats, and has exalted the humble and poor" (Lk 1:52). The mystery here is that God does both of these to the same person. He puts down the mighty and, having humbled him, exalts him. He displaces the center. The history of salvation happens again and again in those who feel the kindness and severity of his touch.

It is not always an easy thing to be a teacher and a monk. These two professions sometimes make conflicting demands on the same person. Discussions of this in my community, and what literature there is on the subject, all tend to focus on the difficulties, the problem of imbalance. We don't hear enough of the experience of balance as a positive grace, and yet it is sometimes given us. I have occasionally found balance between philosophy and liturgy. Excessive preoccupation with liturgy dulls us to experience. We tend toward preconceived emotions, those we feel are appropriate to an occasion. At the other extreme we reflect on our human situation and come too close to it. We lose the fixed point from which we can measure ourselves. Awareness of the mysteries gives us awareness of ourselves. *Noverim me, noverim te.* I think this is part of what the psalmist means as he tells us, over and over again, that meditation on the law is the key to a happy life.

Still, the moments of balance are few. To become aware of grace is to stand convicted as one who needs grace. Celebration of the year of grace occurs on the pilgrimage of those who have not arrived. Every resting place introduces them to a new road.

> Happy are the people whose strength is in you!
> whose hearts are set on the pilgrims' way.

Those who go through the desolate valley
will find it a place of springs;
>   for the early rains have covered it with pools
>   of water.

They will climb from height to height,
>   and the God of gods will reveal himself in Zion
>
>   (Ps 84:5-7).

I

THE CYCLE OF DESIRE
AND KNOWLEDGE

1

The time of desire: Advent

O Lord we wait for you:
   Your memorial name is the desire of our soul.
My soul yearns for you in the night,
   My spirit within me earnestly seeks you (Is 26:8-9).

Desire is a starting place and a meeting place. This is where we begin, wanting things, reaching out, feeling the great strength of our impulses. Since no-one is immune from desire, this is a common ground where I can meet students much younger than I. We know that we desire before we know what we desire. We long for the good which we do not possess. Sometimes we cannot decide what that good is; sometimes we decide, but wrongly. My first question to myself, and to you is, "What do we desire?"

Advent is the time of desire. So is late November. A friend of mine who had been to a Catholic college told me of the scheduled boredom, every Advent, of their chaplain's "eager-longing" sermon. ("Sure we're longing eagerly — longing to finish exams and get out of this place for Christmas vacation . . .") How vivid our short-term goals are! The evening planned; the weekend; the vacation. Faithfully we obey our desires for creature comforts. An Oxford divine at the turn of the century, known for his patristic scholarship and his sumptuous teas, said that as a Christian he believed in an afterlife, but would personally have preferred total extinction. Did he only say what we feel? Satisfy all our immediate wants, and we ask no more . . . .

Then there is passion, the upsurge of physical desire. I share this, too, with the students, although they see me as an apostle of self-denial. Each year, as the seniors read Plato, we discover that pleasure is not the same thing as happiness.[1] In order to have pleasure, says Plato, we must induce some pain, and then relieve it. Pleasure is the return from pain to point zero, the mid-line stasis. Drinking relieves thirst; peristalsis relieves tension. Before we can renew pleasure, we must renew some pain, experience a need. We must again descend below zero to rise up again, and then again down, and up. Plato sees true pleasure as the first step above zero. It is a positive condition of the soul, well being. It cannot be judged by those who have never been there. St. Gregory the Great says that the pleasures of the body are strongly desired but that these desires, once satisfied, disappear. If we overindulge them, they turn to disgust. The pleasures of the soul, by contrast, are scarcely desired at first, but as soon as they are satisfied, the desire increases and continues to grow greater with every satisfaction.[2]

The students hear all this, and they understand, but they

---

[1]Plato, *Republic*, IX. 582-587.

[2]Gregory the Great, *Homiliae in evangelia* (PL 76. 1266 A-B).

keep their counsel. How can Plato's voice be clearly heard over
the din of their own desires?

> Caught in that sensual music, all neglect
> Monuments of unaging intellect.[3]

What is my role to be? Much of the time, it is to say no, to
advise restraint, occasionally to punish self-indulgence. If
Plato's voice is faint as he describes philosophic happiness, my
voice is loud as I enforce the school's requirements. I am no
Socratic figure . . .

> And priests in their gowns were walking their rounds,
> And binding with briars my joys and desires.[4]

During the year of grace I stumbled, as it then seemed to
me, into some conversations with students about desire,
where desire was in fact a meeting place, our common ground.
The first of these began in a term paper. The students, in pairs,
were writing to each other, in this case about uses of the mind.
One of them in a moment of candor discussed his experience
of alcohol and drugs. He is serious about some of his experiences. You cannot really understand, he says to me, since you
haven't tried it. Thinking of Saint Gregory, I agree, but ask
him to try and explain the difference. He speaks, as I half
expect him to, of seeing a higher reality, of revelation. I have to
remember that this is 1979 and that this boy, although one of
the more sophisticated members of his class, may never have
heard of Huxley or Castaneda. It is no longer fashionable, at

---

[3]W. B. Yeats, "Sailing to Byzantium."

[4]William Blake, "The Garden of Love."

his age, to speak of drugs as a spiritual experience. He is speaking directly of what has happened to him.

I can only accept what he says, and perhaps ask a few questions. What is he looking for in these experiences? He himself has eliminated sexual pleasure, and opted for perception of something. He is too intelligent to say that a drug can of itself yield a higher reality, yet too honest to write off the experience he really had. What then? We reach an impasse. I think that what he finds will be determined by what he really is looking for. But what is that? I tell him that he really desires God. He giggles intelligently, which shows that this is quite a new and preposterous idea, but interesting. He does not think of himself as a religious person. Like some of his older brothers and sisters, he has wanted no part of a Catholicism which he identifies with his parents' code of socially acceptable behaviour. Right now, it seems no more likely that he will try Catholicism than that I will try drugs. It is a stand off. During the conversation, both of us have felt threatened, and we respect each other for having had the force to produce that feeling.

It was at about the same time that I had a conversation with another student. Our topic, again, was the paper assigned on uses of the mind. This boy, known more for his charm than self-discipline, had come to ask for suggestions. As I remember, the talk went something like this:

I: You like music, don't you? (My interlocutor is a good jazz player.)

HE: Really.

I: Drugs?

HE: Well, yes, sometimes.

I: And sex?

HE: Well sure, doesn't everyone?

I: Of course. These are all pleasures, and I wonder if there's something that they all have in common, some one reason why you like them all?

HE: I don't know, I've never thought about it. I guess they're exciting; they break the monotony.

I: Of school?

HE: Yes...

I: Of life in general?

HE: I think both.

I: Is that good or bad?

HE: (Self-conscious) I guess, bad?

I: Is it? I mean, is it bad to break monotony? When you do these things, do you think of yourself as escaping from reality?

HE: (laughing) No.

I: I agree. You're not escaping from anything at all, but you want to break out of the monotony of day to day existence.

HE: Yes.

I: So it's like a hamster's wheel, going round and round, and sometimes you get outside of it?

HE: Yes.

I: Then let me ask you this: what is outside?

HE: What do you mean?

I: I mean, you're conscious of something else, you're outside the daily routine. You get high, or maybe it's sexual pleasure. You're outside...

HE: Yes...

I: Well, what is *there*? *What* is outside?

HE: (Now thinking hard.) I don't know, I've never thought

about that. There must be something.

I: Do you believe, or do you think, that there *is* anything outside daily existence?

HE: You mean do I believe in God?

I: If you want to put it that way.

HE: Yes, I believe in God.

I: Do you desire God?

HE: Hm, I don't know. I guess. . .I guess not.

I: Has it ever occurred to you that your desire, for instance, to get high, to break out of the wheel, might really be your desire for God?

HE: (Again thinking hard.) I've just never thought of that. I see what you're saying. Suppose it is? What does that mean?

I: What do you think it means?

HE: That I should turn to God. . .I guess. Yeah. . .

What I hope for in these students, as in myself, is not the diminution of desire but its intensification, the desire for a great happiness which is not satisfied with the round of momentary pleasures. If Advent is the time of longing, it is also the time of *eschaton*, the end of all things. Could there be a desire so momentous that it threatened to burst apart a tidy and comfortable life? We are so familiar with the way this happens in one direction — the well brought-up child whose narrow world of self-restraint is broken open by the discovery of some passion. Can it happen the other way? Can we desire eternal life badly enough that we forget about our creature comforts, our momentary gratifications? This desire can be so strange and so unconventional that it, too, can appear as sin. Jung reports that, as a young child, he was thinking about the cathedral in his city and about God sitting on his golden throne in the clear blue sky. Suddenly he realized with horror that the next thought he was to think on this subject would be a terrible thought, inadmissible, a sin. He would not allow it to happen, although still it waited just outside his consciousness. The struggle went on for days. It seemed inevitable that the thought would happen, but then the child feared damnation for his sin. Finally he decided that God himself was responsible for the thought, even if it was a wicked one, and that God therefore wanted him to be brave. "I gathered up all my courage, as though I were about to leap forthwith into hell-fire, and let the thought come. I saw before me the cathedral, the blue sky. God sits on his golden throne, high above the world — and from the throne an enormous turd falls upon the sparkling new roof, shatters it, and breaks the walls of the cathedral asunder." The boy's happiness was instant and overwhelming. Instead of damnation he had a revelation of God, that God is greater and more powerful than the Church, with its strictures. The "sin" he had feared was the fear, felt from inside that narrowness, of what lies beyond, outside.[5]

I agree with Jung that God gives us our desires, passions, thoughts. We are not to trample them under, or pretend that they do not exist. Neither are we simply to indulge them as they appear. We are to understand our desires, look at them and question them. They entice us and threaten us. To confront our unconscious without giving way to it — this is a path of risk, but also of salvation.[6]

[5]C. G. Jung, *Memories, Dreams, Reflections* (New York: Vintage Books, 1961), pp. 36-41, esp. 39.

[6]See the fine treatment of this theme by a Jungian, James Hillman, in his *Insearch* (New York: Scribner's, 1967), esp. ch. 2, "Inner Life: the Unconscious as Experience."

Is God the true end of desire? Is my monastic life the expression of all my desires? If so, what of my life? What are my desires, and where is my joy? I have questioned my students, but this is their question to me. I often feel that the appearances are against me. After nearly twenty years of monastic life, I have piled up my share of creature comforts, my times of listless distraction at prayer — "If I should count them they would be as the sand of the sea." In spite of all that, I feel a desire and a happiness, feelings of great strength, although they have neither the intoxicating power of passion nor the commanding power of habit. They lie deeper than that, and rule my life. "The love of Christ compels us." The most difficult thing is to explain what it is that compels us to be faithful to it, what it is that we desire.

Some enlightenment on this subject came to me last year at a time when I least expected it. I had agreed to go to a meeting of librarians and be one of several panelists, each of whom would present a few favorite books on psychology and religion. I spoke of Augustine's *Confessions*, Pieper's *Leisure the Basis of Culture*, and De Rougement's *Love in the Western World*. A university professor was there to speak of contemporary authors who have used the thought of Freud for a restatement of Christian values: Norman O. Brown, Tom Driver, Sam Keen, and Peter Schaeffer. He spoke after me, and as he did, I was suddenly brought up short. Referring to my comments about Augustine's theme of the timeless soul, Pieper's emphasis on contemplation, and De Rougement's critique of passion, the speaker said, "Of course, my authors consider people like De Rougement and Pieper as the enemy." I guess that I have always enjoyed oppositions. This one helped me to see our tradition in a sharper light.

This "post-Freudian" Christianity (which is not quite faithful to Freud — but I cannot argue that here) charges traditional spirituality with an excessive concern for the spirit which ignores the full human person and the demands of the body. We are not to repress or deny that part of ourselves which seeks pleasure. Instead, we are to fulfill our own desires, in short, to be ourselves. We are to get rid of dualist, Platonic, guilt-inducing Christianity. Traditional, monastic spirituality is the enemy, the priests in their gowns.

There is, of course, an ethical question here — whether Christians should or should not pursue this philosophy of self-fulfillment. Interesting as that question is, I prefer to ask only this: does this "dionysiac" religiousness really do what is claimed for it? Does it really fulfill, and does it really bring us closer to God?

What is involved, then, is a critique of experience. Our starting point — both sides agree on this — is experience, and we try to see how this will lead us to God. The question is to know what sort of experience will do this for us. My students and I discussed drugs and sex, comparing the desire for these things with desire for God. We did not, however, say that indulgence in sex or drugs would satisfy that desire, or would of itself constitute a religious experience. The post-Freudians seem to claim that it can and does. One side argues for self-denial, the other for self-indulgence, as the best route to true happiness.

If we keep to the pragmatic question — which of these in fact leads to happiness — rather than the moral issue of what we ought to do, some words of Jesus may help: "He who loves his life loses it, and he who hates his life in this world will keep it for eternal life" (Jn 12:25). Self-indulgence is self-defeating.

It always brings us back to ourselves. The fulfillment that we seek is an expansion, a stretching of our narrow limits. Paradoxically, all our attempts at self-fulfillment produce the opposite effect. As long as self is at the center, it always draws everything else back around itself. We fasten our desire on one object after another, only to find that final bad taste of ourselves. At the end of Woody Allen's *Manhattan*, we are not quite sure why we feel pity for the hero as he tells his cassette recorder the things that make life worth living: ". . . the second movement of the Jupiter symphony, Cézanne's apples and pears, Louis Armstrong playing . . . ." At the end of the list he finds "the look on Tracy's face" and, surprised, runs half way across town to try and recapture Tracy, a girl who had been a plaything for his ego. He finds her, and the pathos is that he cannot understand why she no longer cares about him. There is something about self-indulgence which makes joy very hard to find, even at the end of a long run. He who seeks his life will lose it.

And he who loses will find. In his autobiography, *Surprised by Joy*, C. S. Lewis analyzes this second truth in telling of his conversion.[7] His life as an atheist had been a search for the joy which certain childhood experiences had convinced him must exist. And yet, for all his seeking, he could never find it. He solved his problem by making the distinction between a feeling and the object of that feeling. I enjoy the *Jupiter* symphony. The distinction lies between the enjoyment caused by the symphony and the symphony itself. Which of these two, my enjoyment or the symphony, is my primary

[7]C. S. Lewis, *Surprised by Joy* (London: Geoffrey Bles, 1955), pp. 205-215.

concern? The mistake we make is in answering, "the enjoy-ment," for as long as we say that, we are prevented from true enjoyment. If my concern is for my feeling, how can I really get the pleasure of entering into that other world which is Mozart's? The death of a friend saddens me, and the sight of the beloved gladdens me. What I do is to exercise the emotions of sorrow and joy, but these emotions are not, or should not be my primary *concern*. What matters is not my feeling, but those whom I love. One day, then, Lewis realized that his search for joy would always be frustrated because it was just that, the pursuit of a feeling. He would never find joy until he stopped seeking it and sought something else, the true cause of joy. It was then that he began to believe in God.

Why must this paradox be? Why must the search for happiness defeat itself? How can we *not* seek our own happi-ness and why, therefore, must we always be causing our own unhappiness? Some basic reflections show that the paradox is simply a fact of human being. As a person, I am a center of consciousness. In order to be myself I must be conscious, and in order to do that I must be conscious *of* something. All that I am conscious of is other than myself. The one thing of which I cannot be conscious is my own consciousness. If I am aware of myself, it is only to the extent that I objectify certain parts of myself. I can reflect on past actions, look in the mirror, listen to what I'm saying while I'm saying it, and so on. But the "I," the subject which is performing these acts of consciousness, can never be the object of itself, any more than my lips can kiss themselves. To be myself is to be conscious, and to be con-scious is to focus on anything other than myself.

Still, this can't be the whole story. There must be some self-reference. I sense the world around me, the world of others invading my consciousness. Were I to become totally absorbed by these objects around me, I would cease to be aware of myself, cease to be. How can consciousness imply a loss of self and still be the source of my identity?

It was Aquinas who went to the heart of this paradox in his analysis of human knowing.[8] My knowledge of another being depends on my senses, but the senses of themselves do not give me knowledge. I see and hear my friend, but these sights and sounds are not he. The friend I know is not just a friendly image, maintains Aquinas, but the true being of the friend himself. In order for this knowledge to occur, my friend's being must be, must happen within me. Since my friend cannot be physically inside me, this event must be a spiritual one. From the sensory appearances my intellect must abstract a form or act of being. (For Aristotle and Aquinas, the essence of a thing is essentially an *activity* of its being, the activity of form shaping matter.) In order for me to know my friend, therefore, I do two things: I draw form from the sensory appearances of my friend, and then I make of my mind a passive receptor for that form to act upon. My mind, to use a crude analogy, becomes clay to the friend's form. For me to know that friend, my mind must become him. Since, for Aquinas, the mind is not material, it can perform these acts of identification without in fact materially becoming its objects. The mind is *quodammodo omnia* — in a sense all things. It is only by virtue of becoming what it knows that the mind can, in Aquinas' view, really know things as they are.

This is Wordsworth's wise passivity; it is Claudel's *co-naissance*. It is knowledge by becoming, a beautiful activity

---

[8]Thomas Aquinas, *Summa Theologiae* 1.79.

which contains the solution to a spiritual problem. When we reach out with our senses, when we gather information and the senses' own pleasure, there is still no true contact with being as long as we remain the center of our activity. Paradoxically, the moment of becoming can only take place after we bring all our sense information back within ourselves. It is there, within reflection, that we lose our self-centeredness and become united with what is other. The one being that I cannot seek and cannot know, *to* which I cannot be united, is myself. I become myself by exercising my most characteristic activity, knowing, and this means constant identification with other being. To reflect is to abandon my identity for another being, an act by which I discover both that being and myself. He who seeks himself will lose himself; he who seeks others will find himself.

Zen, if I understand it, says the same sort of thing about selfless concentration, except that it is presented as a virtually impossible ideal that we spend a lifetime trying to attain. I couldn't begin to do Zen archery. Even my tennis swing is locked in self-consciousness. What Aquinas does in speaking of knowing is to describe what we all do, all the time. He does not ask us to strive for the unattainable, but simply to appreciate what we already have. Such appreciation comes as a grace.

If you learn to do this in one area of your experience, you will find yourself doing it in others. Of course, we still need saints, the examples of those who have done what we wish we could do; we need to see people who have found themselves by being selfless. We can still learn a great deal by turning to stories of Zen masters, gurus, desert fathers, twice-born athletes, by admiring the sanctity of a Dorothy Day or a Mother

Teresa. The counsels of these heroes are invaluable, but their example shines from a distance. One of my biggest discoveries during the year of grace has been the sanctity of some of our students.

One of them that I knew spent four years here doing things for others. He was popular, and had a gift for organization. He spent hours, over these years, in making student activities happen. He was not unrecognized, in fact he always won elections, but it was virtually impossible to detect the colors of ambition in his manner. He was not a gifted student. In order to achieve a record slightly better than average, he put in long hours completing assignments which others could do in a fraction of the time. He had no reputation for piety, but after a night of studying, would sometimes go into the church and pray in the darkness. He has a simple and direct faith in God. He rarely wastes time, although he never seems busy or hurried. He cares about other people, but does not try to group them around himself. He is totally uninterested in power, although he possessed a great deal of it, and is as free of affectation as anyone I have known. He is full of desire — to do well in college, to have friends, to help others — but has both a selflessness and a sense of self-fulfillment which are inspiring to many of those who knew him. He is not perfect, but his limitations and blunders are as evident as anyone else's. This is exactly what makes his sanctity impressive. It is not striven for, it is given and received.

Advent is the time of desire. Desire is the starting place and the meeting place. What do we desire? Joy, happiness. We have learned to recognize these emotions without knowing their true source. Our society has learned to produce and

market the things which will activate feelings of happiness
—the sex culture, the alcohol and drugs. Here the self-
centered individual tries to make himself happy. That is the
ultimate contradiction. Think of Timothy Leary, beseeching
his followers: "Just be happy!"

"My soul yearns for you in the night . . ." We meet at our
common ground and examine our desires, whatever they may
be — the desire to do another's will or naked ambition, the
desire for another's good or lust. Before any of us can articulate
these desires, we just desire, not knowing what we want.
Everything hinges on the name we give our desire. All names
finally are resolved in one of two, either "I" or "You." If the
happiness we seek has "I" at its center, as so much of our
hedonistic culture would have it, our search is systematically
excluded from its goal. If we desire some "You," some Other to
replace our center, we have a chance. My students read
Augustine: "You have made us for yourself, and our hearts are
restless until they rest in you."[9] They can be told that only
God will make them happy, but they will not understand any
more than I will, if someone just tells them. If we examine our
desires, and see where they lead us — if we examine our
restlessness — we may begin to understand happiness.

The time of desire is also the time of the *eschaton*, the end of
everything. We resist Augustine's saying, finally, not because
we don't understand him but because we do. The student
with whom I had my conversation ended by realizing that
only God could really make him happy, and many others
sense the same thing. All are afraid. All those voices — lust,

---

[9]Augustine, *Confessions* I.I.

ambition, vanity — whisper to us as they whispered to Augustine, "Don't be foolish; you cannot give us up!"[10] The thought of God is the terrible thought which, if we allow it to come to us, will destroy our little world of status and momentary pleasures. We go away sorrowing.

But then we return, and we ask again, "What do we desire?" We will always have desires, please God, and so we can always examine them afresh, perhaps this time to understand God's plan for us. During this year of grace I discovered desire as a common ground, and having met some students upon that ground, I found myself learning from some of them.

There is a great deal to be thankful for.

[10]*Confessions*, VIII.11.

2

The time of the specific: Incarnation

We were just sitting there talking when Peter Maurin came in.

We were just sitting there talking when lines of people began to form, saying, "We need bread. . ."

We were just sitting there talking and people moved in on us. Let those who can take it, take it . . .

We were just sitting there talking and someone said, "Let's all go live on a farm . . ."

It all happened while we sat there talking, and it is still going on.[1]

God surprises us. When we were least expecting it, something happened. Desire reaches upward, seeking the infinite. God gives us the good we never dared ask for, never dreamed of; he gives us the finite. The world lies in stillness, hesitant after the prayers of all holy men and women for a Savior, for the coming of God — and God responds. How? Oh, nothing

[1]Dorothy Day, *The Long Loneliness* (New York: Image, 1959), pp. 276-277.

much. Someone arrived at night. A child was born. Then they left. We were sitting around. Someone came in. That's how it all began.

It is a fact of our culture that we are less familiar with concrete and finite symbols of the divine than we are with themes of the infinite and unknown. Allen Tate's "angelic imagination" is that longing for the infinite which tries to extend itself infinitely, approximating to the superhuman and so *becoming* the infinite which it seeks.[2] The poet in his rapture and the lover in her ecstasy seek the attainment of their goals at the end of a long leap. The cultural equivalent of "angelic" is "romantic." In some authors, such as Poe and Baudelaire, it becomes a mysticism of the senses. The desire for the infinite, pursued in specifically sensual terms, wants to go anywhere out of the world, be it heaven or hell. Following our reflections on desire, it should come as no surprise that sensual mysticism ends, as some of its practitioners admit, in hell. As long as we achieve ecstasy, Baudelaire concludes, what does it matter whether we are angels or demons?[3]

The *poète maudit* is a very late descendant of an old line. Romantic sensibility appeared in religion well before its appearance in literature. The sixteenth-century debate on justification went to the heart of the matter. The first romantics were the reformers who objected to Catholic piety as a system of dead works. Catholics, they claimed, sought salvation by performing a set of works which were extrinsic to the concerns of religious being. What did it profit a man to recite set prayers, give sums of money to the church, fast, travel to

[2] Allen Tate, *The Forlorn Demon* (Chicago: Regnery, 1953), pp. 32-78.

[3] Charles Baudelaire, "Hymne à la beauté."

certain shrines? Would any of these prescribed activities "cleanse the conscience from dead works?" The faithful might do anything they were told to by the religious authorities, but still remain inwardly unchanged, still estranged from the God they were vainly trying to placate. The reformers looked on Catholic piety as many Christians today would on an Indian rain dance.

What was the alternative? If we reject an outward justification, we will opt for an inward one (especially if we tend to be controversialists, as the reformers did). At this point, no word from an authority and no exterior works can help me find salvation. No one can tell me I am saved. Only through faith can I tell this to myself. Justification by faith, seen as a purely inward process, ends with the proposition, "I am saved if I feel saved." This, in essense, is the romantic or subjectivist principle in religion.

It is well to remember that such "principles" are scarcely ever found embodied in their pure state. Other-directed Catholics of the past were not mere religious robots. They too had inward, spiritual lives. Inner-directed reformers also recognized outward authorities and had little toleration for those early enthusiasts, like Muntzer, who allowed their feelings to guide them in all things. Despite this, the subjective principle has, since the Reformation, become an inseparable part of our modern religious outlook. We invoke it unconsciously. Our ancestors of the sixteenth century lived in fear of divine retribution and worked out their salvation with diligence. Not we — we have feelings, good and bad, about ourselves. We justify ourselves, knowing somehow that God is too nice to condemn people as nice as we. If we are comfortable with ourselves, we may be comfortable with God. To be sure, there have been dissident voices, such as that of Karl Barth, sternly warning us that God's ways are not our ways, but these tend to be drowned out in the greater romantic hubbub: "If it feels good to me, it is good."

Catholics have jumped on the romantic bandwagon for a well-earned ride. After all, they laid the roadway for it as early as the middle ages with their increasing emphasis on "sensible devotion." G. L. Prestige has traced the history of what he calls "divine eros," devotion to the humanity of Christ, which places ever greater emphasis on the worshiper's own feelings.[4] If C. S. Lewis is right, this is the great mistake. In the romantic period itself, Chateaubriand argues for the truth of the Christian religion from the subjective emotions of transcendence awakened in us by Gothic arches and ancient music.[5] The literature of Catholic devotion over the last two centuries pays an unparalleled homage to sentiment. While many present-day Catholics applaud the change in musical taste from "Mother Dear, Oh Pray for Me" to the latest guitar ballad, others note that there is still a common denominator of taste which approves of all that provokes religious emotions, turns people on, makes them feel saved. I am far from criticizing emotions as such in religion. Many valid religious movements today are very emotional; in a subsequent chapter I will tell how I have been helped by one of these. I become critical only when I see feelings become the measure of all things. A person's first experience of such feelings is sometimes referred to as "getting saved," as though the emotional experience were itself the redemptive event. A streak of intolerance sometimes

[4]G. L. Prestige, *Fathers and Heretics* (London: SPCK, 1954), pp. 180-207.

[5]François-René de Chateaubriand, *Le génie du christianisme.*

appears, a tendency to view more humdrum Christians as whitened sepulchres. Average churchgoers may, indeed, view themselves as such. One senses a loss of nerve among many of the more conventional Christians, a doubt whether simple performance of religious duties is getting them anywhere. Thus the subjectivist principle is recognized, even if only tacitly, on all sides.

This sketch of religious romanticism would not be complete without drawing in the fringe, that galaxy of fads for which cultivation of the turned-on consciousness is an end in itself. All of these activities, pure as they may be in themselves, have been marketed very profitably. There is also the beatific drug. Invoking the writings of Huxley and his followers, and fortified with a whole culture of bogus religiosity, sharp people for some time now have been intercepting young people like my own students, whose desire for God and his bliss could be profitably channeled into desire for a drug and *its* bliss. My counter-offensive, with its attempt to channel desire for drugs into desire for God, makes me feel like the mouse that roared. How can my religion compete with this fascinating cult and its instant mysticism? Feel saved? Better than that — feel in heaven![6] As far as religious romanticism is concerned, it really doesn't matter what you say, or what is really there. All that matters is how you feel. Desire mounts up and up, infinitely. It becomes infinite, even without encountering an object, and so becomes its own object. Angel or demon, it finds its joy in itself.

[6]The bogus claims of drug mysticism are submitted to the scrutiny of R. C. Zaehner in his *Mysticism, Sacred and Profane* (Oxford: Clarendon, 1957), and *Zen, Drugs and Mysticism* (New York: Pantheon, 1972).

So surprising is the Incarnation that it seems to contradict desire, as the symbolic imagination contradicts the angelic. The angelic attempt to know God by becoming divine is doomed to failure because, as Tate points out, "the human intellect cannot reach God as essence, only God as analogy."[7] We cannot get so high as to become God, but we can understand God in our own terms when he gets so low as to be us. Taking Dante as representative of the symbolic imagination, Tate shows that it is not by leaping into the infinite, but by standing where he is that Dante sees the divine light, reflected in an earthly mirror. It is not through a mystical unhinging of the senses that we will reach God, but by the means which he himself has chosen.

The way of analogy is the way of the symbol, a humble thing which points beyond itself. It is a way of grace. What human invention could contrive that the most familiar things — light, water, wind, bread — would give to man saving knowledge of God? They do because they are given to us, not sought. They are not man's work, and they shape his life. Then comes the second gift. From the elements are taken smaller symbols, some particular things or events which carry the divine, transform our lives. These are the totally unexpected symbols, given to one man alone.

> To see a World in a grain of sand,
> And a Heaven in a wild flower,
> Hold Infinity in the palm of your hand,
> And eternity in an hour.[8]

[7]Tate, *The Forlorn Demon*, p. 77.
[8]William Blake, "Auguries of Innocence."

Dry the pool, dry concrete, brown edged,
And the pool was filled with water out of sunlight,
And the lotus rose, quietly, quietly,
The surface glittered out of heart of light,
And they were behind us, reflected in the pool.
   Then a cloud passed, and the pool was empty.
Go, said the bird, for the leaves were full of children,
Hidden excitedly, containing laughter.
Go, go, go, said the bird: human kind
Cannot bear very much reality.[9]

"We were all sitting there talking when someone came in." When God entered our world as man, it was not what we expected. The virgin is surprised, even shocked at the news; Joseph does not understand. The child is born and grows, and still they do not understand. If only we could share their lack of understanding, hear the story as though for the first time! Mary hears it, and is troubled. We hear the same message of the angel and, summoning our appropriate Christmas emotions, are not the least bit troubled. We may dissect the story with the scissors of biblical criticism and put it back together with the latest theological paste, but somewhere we lose the terrible reality of a childbirth which is that of God. We know the story before we hear it. Like Herod's astrologers, we know everything about the Nativity except the way to the stable. We see a *creche*, and forget how this child cried, and needed to be fed and have his diapers changed. (How long, I wonder, were swaddling clothes kept on?) We have our romantic stable, forgetting what horse barns and cow barns are like. Where shall we find the greatest symbol of all, God in human

[9]T. S. Eliot, *Four Quartets*, "Burnt Norton."

form? Make it a cow barn, or make it a poor kitchen with dirty dishes in the sink, a cracked draughty window and a bare light bulb, and make the child howl for the cold and lack of food, and when you see, you worship, because you are looking at God, the maker of heaven and earth and all that is in them.

Mary is troubled, and asks, "How can this be?" She hears the answer, and is still troubled. She asks, "How can this happen to me?" Even if she could accept that this God should take flesh in a human womb, how can she accept that it be her womb? This is the moment of incarnation, because to take flesh means to take some specific flesh. Some of our bitterest struggles are with the specific, the here and now. Why me? Why did I alone have to suffer, or why did I alone survive? Is there a reason why I was born as I was, or is it just chance? Why this time and place? "Can any good come out of Nazareth?" Did you bring me all this way just to bathe in that dirty river? — Yes, Naaman, this river. The one you see. When sick, I feel that any other pain or disease would be preferable to *this* one. When forced to do an unwelcome duty, I feel that I could do anything for the Lord, but why this absurd task, why these impossible people? The present moment is the only time, and where I am is the only place where I can encounter God. The God of my mind is an idol, ready to be worshiped when I call good what feels good, when I make myself the center of my unreal life. The real God takes flesh and speaks to me in circumstances which are not of my choice. The money I cannot spend as I would like is gold at Jesus' feet. Jesus is born in the house I clean, or the office where I work, in the place where I am constrained to be. "Let it be done to me according to your will." That is living in the here and now.

Jesus was born in a specific body and in a specific time and place. He thus becomes the foundation of the sacramental life of Christians, the life of the here and now, of the specific. What did Christ come to embrace and save, if not our human *karma*? "The sacrament of the present moment" is simply the imitation of Christ. The life of Jesus is the doing of God's will from moment to moment in the often humble tasks we find before us. This tiresome person to talk with, this cold to endure, this financial worry, this evening at home, this sin to be sorry for — these are the sacraments which are given to us by God. They are the stable, the flesh which becomes God's.

We have a deep resistance to incarnation — at least I do. It was only after I started the monastic life that I realized how strong this resistance was. One day in mid-October of my first year, I suddenly stopped in the middle of mopping the church floor, and thought, "This is absurd! All my friends are in graduate school, or beginning a career, and what am I doing? This makes no sense." It was a real crisis of vocation: I almost left on the spot. Somehow, during those days, I decided not to go, just to persevere a little longer. The storm passed, and I have never really had any serious doubts about my vocation since.

I still resist. Part of me calls this the sacrament of God's presence and part of me calls it a bourgeois spirituality of the *status quo*. What place does this attitude hold for creativity, originality, breaking old patterns and finding new ones? What about inspirations and charisms? In answer to my own question, I note that the Incarnation itself was a fairly drastic departure from everyday routine, and that it was the work of the Holy Spirit. St. Ambrose points out that Mary was simply going about her business when the angel greeted her and the

Holy Spirit overshadowed her.[10] In its most perfect form, the sacrament of the present moment means total availability to the inspiration of the Spirit. The reason we despise the here and now as a way to God is that we do not believe, at bottom, that God would ever, or could ever, visit us in such drab surroundings. It is only in the heightened atmosphere of a group meeting or some "peak moment" that we expect the Spirit to move us. What if we, like the Blessed Virgin, were completely open to grace in our daily tasks? Perfect openness to God means that we do not reach out to force his hand. Mary's receptive attitude is the basis for her ability to conceive: *Prius concepit mente quam corpore;* She conceived in her mind before she did so in her womb.[11] To be unselfconsciously absorbed in our duty as being the will of God is to have the greatest availability to the charisms of the Holy Spirit.

This gospel of specificity is a hard saying. It is no light matter that we should tie ourselves down to a here and now, especially when it comes to commitments. In our culture we are mobile, protean. We require frequent changes of surroundings and occupation. Our sense of commitment is sometimes intense, but often short-lived. Marriage is an incarnation, a cleaving to some specific flesh — "bone of my bones and flesh of my flesh." In choosing to cleave to each other, two people choose not to cleave to anyone else. Every explicit choice for implies many implicit choices against. In this case, the choice is for life. As the divorce rate mounts, we wonder if this isn't too much to ask. Two people know how they feel now; they do not know how they will feel in five or ten years. How can

[10]Ambrose: "Disce virginem moribus," *Liber 2 in Lucam* (PL 15. 1557).

[11]Leo the Great, *Sermo 21 de Nativitate Domini* (PL 54.191).

they be specific about the future? Specificity is, after all, in the here and now, and the future is neither of these. The same uncertainty arises when young people consider religious life. It is one thing to feel the call to monastic life and quite another thing to make vows, write a blank check with all the heres and nows to be filled in later and payment always to be made. I feel like it now, but how can I be sure that I always will be able to honor that commitment?

We can never, of course, be sure. There is no way to predict future states of mind. What we often forget, though, is that future states of mind proceed from present ones. Every decision made now contributes to future decisions. Every act of faithlessness contributes to future faithlessness. Every betrayal weakens my trust in myself. Every day's acts weave more strands into a texture which will result, ultimately, in the stuff we are made of. There are few decisions and acts so moment- ous as of themselves to change the course of our lives, but the accumulation of many small decisions and acts does determine our course. Paradoxically, the only way to be sure of a future faithfulness is by being faithful now. We cannot know the future, but we can help to build it. Every acceptance of a here and now — "let it be done to me according to your will" — is also an act of trust in the God who gave me that here and now, and who will give me all succeeding moments. Faithfulness is a question of trust, and trust can only be established by actions, by venturing to do the thing which is at hand.

The man of God appears to the world as a living paradox. He thinks there is something special about his dirty river. He is known to be nothing more than a carpenter's son, and yet he stands up and prophesies. She touches God by changing diapers, a God who looks down from his throne on high to behold the lowly, to lift them up and set down the mighty. This paradox of high and low also stretches out horizontally, across time. God is kind and severe; he condemns and saves. We accept incarnation, being tied down to the specific, and in this we find freedom. In humble details we find openness to the impulses of the Spirit. Faithful in a few things, we are set over much. We are tenacious in duty and flexible in grace.

Or such is the ideal; the reality is imperfectly attained, if ever. We are always so busy with desire and ambition, with the pursuit of freedom and happiness, that we fail to notice the desired goal lying, not in the escape from our burdens, but in our acceptance of them.

> I struck the board, and cry'd, No more!
>   I will abroad.
> What? Shall I ever sigh and pine?
> My lines and life are free, free as the rode,
>   Loose as the winds, as large as store.
>   Shall I be still in suit?
> Have I no harvest but a thorn
> To let me bloud, and not restore
> What I have lost with cordiall fruit?
>   Sure there was wine
> Before my sighs did drie it. There was corn
>   Before my tears did drown it.
> Is the yeare only lost to me?
>   Have I no bayes to crown it?
> No flowers, no garlands gay? All blasted?
>   All wasted?
> Not so, my heart! But there is fruit,
>   And thou hast hands.

Recover all thy sigh-blown age
On double pleasures. Leave thy cold dispute
Of what is fit and not. Forsake thy cage,
    Thy rope of sands,
Which pettie thoughts have made, and made to thee
    Good cable, to enforce and draw,
            And be thy law,
    While thou didst wink and wouldst not see,
            Away! Take heed!
            I will abroad.
Call in thy death's head here. Tie up thy fears.
    He that forbears
    To suit and serve his need
    Deserves his load.
But as I rav'd and grew more fierce and wilde
        At every word,
    Me thoughts I heard one calling, *Childe!*
        And I reply'd *My Lord.*[12]

There could be no better words for the dialogue of Advent and Christmas. First vaulting desire, then genuflecting fulfillment. First the calling out of the search, then the hush of being found by the thing sought for. It was there all the time, beneath us. First we rise to our desires, then we stoop to a child.

How can we compare these two motions? Our most exalted flights are pitiful in comparison with God's gentle self-humbling. The strength of angelic ecstasy cannot equal the lowly power of God made man, this particular child. The

[12]George Herbert, "The Collar."

Incarnation is Emmanu-el, God with us, always closer than we could have managed to be by our own efforts. "Do not say in your heart, 'Who will ascend into heaven?' (that is, to bring Christ down). . . . But what does it say? The word is near you, on your lips and in your heart . . ." (Rom 10:6-8).

"We were all sitting there talking when someone came in." The Incarnation is the surprise which changes everything, which fulfills all my hopes even while contradicting them. I had so many dreams for myself, so many exalted visions. Now I discover that my wildest aspiration could never encompass that divinity which is contained in the smallest circumstance of the here and now. I had lived on my imagination, trying to be something I fancied to be wonderful, worshiping a God of my creation. All the time the Lord was there, inviting me to bend myself to a humbler reality. How can I thank him enough for the moment, for the year of grace, for the time when I realized that he is here, with me, here and now, in this place, in what I am?

> But as I rav'd and grew more fierce and wilde
>   At every word,
>
> Me thoughts I heard one calling, *Childe!*
>   And I reply'd, *My Lord.*

3

The time of meeting: Epiphany

Since, tho' he is under the world's splendor and wonder,
His mystery must be instressed, stressed;
For I greet him the days I meet him, and bless when I
understand.[1]

With epiphany, or "manifestation," the first cycle is completed. Desire is something we do; incarnation is something God does. Epiphany is something we both do: it is showing and seeing, it is meeting.

How can this happen? We look for God, and he comes, but not as we thought. Or we wait for God, and he does not come at all. He looks for us, and draws near, but we have other things at hand, and cannot be bothered. Or we come to the rendez-vous, and he is there, but it seems impossible really to meet, so far apart are we in every way. I believe in the Incarnation, I keep the commandments, I listen to God's word, I come to the Eucharist, and still I feel God's absence more

---

[1] Gerard Manley Hopkins, "The Wreck of the Deutschland."

than his presence. What chance is there for true meeting, true understanding?

We all feel akin to Beckett's hobos, Vladimir and Estragon, waiting for a Godot who will not show himself, unable in their waiting even to meet each other. Both the isolation and the fruitless waiting are part of the same absurdity. A meeting with Godot and real meeting with each other would amount to the same thing, a breakthrough from delusion to reality. To put it another way, the happiness promised us is already here for those who can reach out and take it. The Incarnation has happened, but who recognizes the child? Why are there so few? Three wise men come from the East, while the local wise men and rulers plot murder. At a hard saying, many followers of Jesus take flight. We know our vaulting desires. We have heard of the lowering of God in the flesh. At what point can we fall down and worship this flesh? Where is the grace for that? "He was in the world, and the world was made through him, yet the world knew him not. He came to his own home, and his own people received him not" (Jn 1:10-11).

Can theology speak of meeting? It can speak of man and his desire; it can speak of God, and the divine acts which have been revealed to man. Here, though, is a different matter. Each meeting between God and a person is a unique event. Who is like God? If I experience God as God, he is the absolute. There is no-one like him, and there is no experience to which I can compare this. The faith of Abraham, Kierkegaard tells us, has nowhere to turn, no other situation to which it can compare itself. The individual meets the absolute, in an absolute relation. The meeting with God is not like anything else. What can we say about it?[2]

[2]Soren Kierkegaard, *The Fear and Trembling.*

Some of the most famous meetings with God are indeed opaque to our minds. Who can understand Paul's conversion? Or the calling of Matthew? After following Augustine through all the arguments that led him to faith, we feel excluded from his struggle in the garden, from really hearing a child's voice saying, "Take it and read it." Can we share the experience of Charles de Foucauld? What would we do if a priest ordered us, "*Confessez-vous,*" as did Father Huvelin to Foucauld, after so many dissolute years?

If we cannot understand these privileged moments, we can at least understand much of what led up to them. We can recognize ourselves in Foucauld and Augustine: if not in their conversions, at least in their sinfulness. We can listen to their stories, and think of our own. Epiphanies are stories: narratives which lead to something seen. By listening to the stories of others, we can come to partial understanding of their epiphanies. There is only one story that we will truly understand — our own — and we will not be able to convey the full understanding of it to others. We can only point to what we see.

While the meeting itself is a private matter, many of the roads leading to that encounter are not. As in all theologies, the possibility of this story theology depends on certain presuppositions. We will have no story to tell if our view of the world is such as to exclude, *a priori,* the possibility of our meeting God. Two points of view, although opposed to each other, are united in holding to such an exclusion.

The first of these will not allow that meeting with God is possible, because it will not allow for anything which is out of the natural order. I am waiting for a sociologist to write a study explaining why so many young people in schools and colleges

today are doctrinaire determinists. Is it the influence of technology, the orthodoxies of their teachers, or the excessive
organization of their lives by their parents and their society? A
student whose life is dominated by a prosperous and over-
solicitous father told me that he has a fantasy that everyone he
meets, even the random panhandler who asks for a quarter, are
all in his father's employ, all arranged in a studied pattern of
influence. The fantasy leads to visions of central offices of
multiple TV screens and James Bond characters giving hand
signals from the roofs of buildings: "He's turning uptown at
79th. . . ." The implicit view behind this daydream is that
the world is a closed system governed by fixed natural,
economic, and sociological laws, one in which there will be no
chance for significant personal creativity or spontaneity. With
this assumption comes a sense of personal futility, the hope-
lessness of trying to make any really important changes in the
world.

The greatest irony implicit in this view is its reason for
rejecting belief in divine providence. If you look at the world
through determinist-colored spectacles, you will see God as
the great puppeteer, the greatest determiner of them all,
looking at all the screens, pulling all the switches. The extent
to which this view is ingrained in some minds can be seen by
the impossibility of convincing people that, just because God
knows everything, it does not follow that he therefore controls
everything. Knowledge is control, they say, and aver that the
coexistence of all knowledge and maximum freedom is absurd.
Be that as it may, this deterministic God, having been
imagined, is rejected, for the simple reason that he is not
needed. The switches have already been pulled; God has
nothing further to do. We have the DNA molecule, we have

the machinations of the big business cartels, we have the laws of stimulus and response. God, said La Place to Napoleon, is a hypothesis for which there is no need. La Place's theories have been discarded, but others have taken their place. We still pursue the chimera of thinking that, with just a little more data and know-how, we will be able to predict all things. Those who disbelieve in God on these grounds would be religious fanatics if belief were thought to yield this predictive key.

The counterpart to determinism is the view which holds the only law in the world to be that of random chance. Quantum mechanics and post-Darwinian evolutionary theory emphasize randomness. General laws are only good predictions, and there is no telling what will happen to any given particle or member of the species. Statistical probability, instead of rational law, appears to govern our lives. The overriding idea, that this is an irrational process, hangs heavy. A film, *The Deerhunter*, gives us Russian roulette as a symbol of fate, of a blind absurdity which broods over the lives of people struggling to be sane in the face of great odds. An isolated particle, the experiencing individual, is not at home in his world. It is a game of chance with no *telos*, no ordering to a final goal. All other people, all moments of time are equally fragmented. There is no context in which to compare one thing to another, nothing except the individual. Desires or hates are felt, and indulged. If you have an experience which you call "spiritual" or "religious," I can make nothing of it, unless the same thing should happen to me. I can infer nothing from your experience, or even from mine. The events of my life happen as they happen, without any ultimate significance.

There is an important sense in which both of these views

agree. Both deny that there is a purpose, a goal toward which
things work. Ever since the abandonment of Aristotelian
science in the sixteenth century, the exclusion of teleology, the
question of purpose, from science has been one of the most
cherished dogmas of thought. When examining the physical
world, the one question we may not ask is, "Why?" Now if
there really is no purpose in nature, it makes little difference
whether you look at things in terms of randomness or in terms
of an order rigidly determined by prior causes. If the question
of meaning, the "why," is excluded, you will conclude that the
world we live in is absurd, and that the structures of thought
which we so strenuously impose on it are quite arbitrary. The
rules will hold only until the game is over. This is not the sort
of world I can reflect on, in which I can find rational patterns
as evidence of God. This is not the sort of world in which I can
expect to find some privileged moments of absolute value, of
which I can say that I felt the touch of God, a touch which
gave meaning to all the other moments of my life.

Secularists, whether determinists or not, show a lack of
self-knowledge in supposing that they have done away with
blind faith. The idea of explaining human development by
random mutations and natural selection was once a theory.
Now many hold it as an irreformable dogma. A young and
brilliant friend of mine has examined this theory indepen-
dently of any religious assumptions and finds it untenable on
purely rational grounds. He tried to discuss his ideas with
college professors, but got no hearing. Now he mentions these
ideas only in private, to friends. He is a heretic to secular
orthodoxy, and while talking to him recently I had my first
experience of how a religious heretic may have felt in other
days. I can't imagine a more rigid orthodoxy than one which

believes miracles do not happen because they cannot happen. Exegetes of this persuasion have attempted to rewrite the New Testament according to their faith. What did and didn't happen turns out to be what we, with our superior knowledge, know can and can't happen. Whatever we "know" (that is, believe piously) can't happen, we call myth, and reject. Seldom has the Word of God been so tightly bound by dogmatic presuppositions.

The net result of such prejudices is the sin against the Holy Spirit, the one unpardonable sin. This is despair, the absolute refusal to suppose that God could ever do what God in fact is about to do. To blaspheme, that is to corrupt the statement of what God *has done* or *is*, is forgivable. God's activity is none the less for that. All other sin, all harm done to others, is forgiveable. God can always change us. But to oppose what God is *about* to do and what, in his love for our freedom, he can only do *with us*, quite prevents God from acting. If we have decided that meeting with God cannot happen, then it will not, since meeting requires two. And if God cannot act, we cannot be forgiven.

Of course, not even secular orthodoxy can keep God from acting in this world. That is why there are such things as the miracles of Lourdes, offenses to the secular mind, which simply will not go away. There is still a remnant of the faithful who believe that, with God, all things are possible. "Master, we toiled all night and took nothing! But at your word I will let down the nets" (Lk 5:5). At a sign, the Magi set out, found the child, and returned to their kingdoms. They might well have returned to their kingdoms having found nothing, but the one thing they could not do was to remain where they were. Epiphany is meeting, but there will be no meeting unless we freely come to the appointed place. There are also those who come and wait, long and alone, like Vladimir and Estragon. They are disappointed, but they keep faith, and the possibility of meeting sustains them from day to day.

An epiphany is a story, or rather a story leading to a tableau, the picture of an instant which, no matter how hard we try to freeze it on our life's stage, passes too quickly for us to capture. Such moments are not necessarily "religious," in the conventional sense of the word. The young man who had the following experience thought of it solely in terms of nature (although he subsequently became a Christian):

> One day during my last term at school I walked out alone in the evening and heard the birds singing in that full chorus song, which can only be heard at that time of the year at dawn or at sunset. I remember now the shock of surprise with which the sound broke on my ears. It seemed to me that I had never heard the birds singing before and I wondered whether they sang like this all the year round and I had never noticed it. As I walked on I came upon some hawthorn trees in full bloom and again I thought that I had never seen such a sight or experienced such sweetness before. If I had been brought suddenly among the trees of the Garden of Paradise and heard a choir of angels singing I could not have been more surprised. I came to where the sun was setting over the playing fields. A lark rose suddenly from the ground beside the tree by which I was standing and poured out its song over my head, and then sank still singing to rest. Everything then grew still as the sunset faded and the veil of dusk began to cover the earth. I remember now the feeling of awe which came over me. I felt inclined to kneel on the ground, as though I had been standing in the presence of an angel; and I

hardly dared to look on the face of the sky, because it seemed as though it was but a veil before the face of God.

These are the words with which I tried many years later to express what I had experienced that evening, but no words can do more than suggest what it meant to me. It came to me quite suddenly, as it were out of the blue, and now that I look back on it, it seems to me that it was one of the decisive events of my life.[3]

Often the circumstances of enlightenment are far less idyllic. Salinger's Buddy Glass finds his in a supermarket:

I was standing at the meat counter, waiting for some rib lamb chops to be cut. A young mother and her little girl were waiting around, too. The little girl was about four, and, to pass the time, she leaned her back against the glass showcase and stared up at my unshaven face. I told her she was about the prettiest little girl I'd seen all day. Which made sense to her; she nodded. I said I'd bet she had a lot of boy friends. I got the same nod again. I asked her how many boy friends she had. She held up two fingers. "Two!" I said. "That's a lot of boy friends. What are their names, sweetheart?" Said she, in a piercing voice, "*Bobby and Dorothy.*" I grabbed my lamb chops and ran . . . The deeper I get into this goddam letter, the more I lose the courage of my convictions. But I swear to you that I had a perfectly communicable little vision of truth (lamb-chop division) this afternoon the very instant that child told me her boy friends' names were Bobby and Dorothy. Seymour once said to me — in a crosstown bus, of all places — that all legitimate religious study *must* lead to unlearning the differences, the illusory differences,

[3]Bede Griffiths, *The Golden String* (New York: P. J. Kenedy and Sons), pp. 9-10.

between boys and girls, animals and stones, day and night, heat and cold. That suddenly hit me at the meat counter, and it seemed a matter of life and death to drive home at seventy miles an hour to get a letter off to you. Oh, God, how I wish I'd grabbed a pencil right there in the supermarket and not trusted the roads home.[4]

It is comforting to me, as one who has to preach, to find that such moments can also occur during sermons:

I happen to believe in God because here and there over the years certain things happened. No one particular untoward thing happened, just certain things. To be more accurate, the things that happened never really were quite certain and hence, I suppose, their queer power.

At twenty-seven, living alone in New York trying with no success to write a novel and in love with a girl who was not in love with me, I went to hear a famous preacher preach one morning although I had no idea at the time that he was famous and went only on impulse — I was not a churchgoer — because his church was next door. . . .

He said that. . .this coronation of Jesus in the believer's heart took place among confession — I thought, yes, yes, confession — and tears, he said — I thought tears, yes, perfectly plausible that the coronation of Jesus in the believing heart should take place among confession and tears. And then with his head bobbing up and down so that his glasses glittered, he said in his odd, sandy voice, the voice of an old nurse, that the coronation of Jesus took place among confession and tears and then, as God was and is my witness, *great laughter*, he said.

[4]J. D. Salinger, *Franny and Zoey* (Boston: Little, Brown and Company, 1955), pp. 63-64, 67-68.

Jesus is crowned among confession and tears and great laughter, and at the phrase *great laughter*, for reasons that I have never satisfactorily understood, the great wall of China crumbled and Atlantis rose up out of the sea, and on Madison Avenue, at 73rd Street, tears leapt from my eyes as though I had been struck across the face.[5]

It sometimes happens that the most crucial occasions have nothing dramatic about them at all. It can only be said that there is a point after which things are not as they were before. C. S. Lewis tells how, after lengthy debate and consideration of his atheism, the turning point came during a bus ride.

The odd thing was that before God closed in on me, I was in fact offered what now appears a moment of wholly free choice. In a sense. I was going up Headington Hill on the top of a bus. Without words and (I think) almost without images, a fact about myself was somehow presented to me. I became aware that I was holding something at bay, or shutting something out. Or, if you like, that I was wearing some stiff clothing, like corsets, or even a suit of armour, as if I were a lobster. I felt myself being, there and then, given a free choice. I could open the door or keep it shut; I could unbuckle the armour or keep it on. Neither choice was presented as a duty; no threat or promise was attached to either, though I knew that to open the door or to take off the corset meant the incalculable. The choice appeared to be momentous but it was also strangely unemotional. I was moved by no desires or fears. In a sense I was not moved by anything. I chose to open, to unbuckle, to loosen the rein. I say, "I chose," yet it did not really seem possible to do the

[5]Frederick Buechner, *The Alphabet of Grace* (New York: Seabury, 1970), pp. 43-44.

opposite. On the other hand, I was aware of no motives. You could argue that I was not a free agent, but I am more inclined to think that this came nearer to being a perfectly free act than most that I have ever done. Necessity may not be the opposite of freedom, and perhaps a man is most free when, instead of producing motives, he could only say, "I am what I do." Then came the repercussion on the imaginative level. I felt as if I were a man of snow at long last beginning to melt. The melting was starting in my back — drip-drip and presently trickle-trickle. I rather disliked the feeling.[6]

Everyone has his own epiphanies. I reach back to find mine, hoping you will reach back to find yours.

During the war my family spent a summer at Edgartown, in a house on Tower Hill. From there you look across the harbor, to the lighthouse at the other end of the town. To me, a very small child, that seemed like the other end of the world. One day I was taken for a walk, through the town, and to the other side as far as the lighthouse. There is no happiness quite like emerging out of a little shell, into a new reality. No great emotion was attached to this day, but I have never forgotten it.

Somewhere in my childhood comes an image of a holy man. Did I read about him, see his picture, or dream of him? Now, but I think then as well, the image is very indistinct. He is old and gentle, has a beard, and lives in a small room. As I come into his presence, I am filled with deep awe and great peace. I never remember his saying anything, nor can I remember any specific time that I thought of him, but his existence was important.

[6]C. S. Lewis, *Surprised by Joy*, pp. 211-212.

One evening at school — I think I was 15 at the time — I was walking back to my dormitory. It was spring and it had been raining. There was a warm, wet wind, a last glow of red in the sky, and a chase of vast clouds. Perhaps I thought of the hymn words,

> His chariots of wrath the deep thunderclouds form,
> And dark is his path on the wings of the storm.

I had no thought of God, but my heart was lifted up and it seemed to me that this might be the end of the world. The clouds could carry us all off, time could end, and there would be nothing more to say. It was terrible, and yet exhilarating. When I stepped indoors, the feeling immediately vanished, remaining only in memory.

When students ask me how I became a monk, I say truthfully that it began when, at the age of sixteen, I first fell in love, and not because this was a sad occurrence, but because it was a happy one, a time of grace. Prior to this, the character I had made for myself at school was a brittle one, a sharp and arrogant shell of wit. To fall in love was to begin my own long, slow melting — drip-drip and trickle-trickle. I never chose to dissolve in this way; it just began to happen. Two instances come to mind.

My girl friend and I are on that trolley which still, I hope, conveys its passengers from Dorchester, through a cemetery, to Milton Lower Mills. On the same car is another boy, a few years younger than I, one of the school oddities. He is loud, always in trouble, vulgar. It seems clear that he will not make it through the whole four years. I start talking to him, teasing him in a patronizing sort of way, less from malice than from habit, putting him down and exalting myself. After he gets off, the girl turns on me: "How can you be so horrible?" She is really angry, and I am shocked, but before she has finished I have seen myself as I really am, not as I imagine myself.

It is Christmas vacation, and I am at home in New York City. I am walking up Fifth Avenue, thinking about a person I really care for. She has some worries and concerns which now concern me, problems I would like to help her solve, but cannot. I turn out of the cold for a brief visit to St. Patrick's Cathedral; it is a place I have always enjoyed visiting, a place both awesome and friendly. I kneel down, and suddenly am overwhelmed by the thought that there *is* something I can do. For perhaps the first time in my life, I experience a serious and whole-hearted desire to pray.

Plato describes love between two people as an initiation into the mysteries of highest reality.[7] Human love is the first step, the first softening of the heart. For me at sixteen, the grace consisted in this, that I began to see a particular love not as an end in itself, but as a participation in some greater Love, something I began to see only in glimpses, but which I knew lay ahead, still to be attained. I would go away, lose old friends and find new ones, and still that love would beckon, ever more desirable.

I spent the summer between school and college traveling in Europe with my parents. Starting from Lucerne one day, we went by boat half way down the lake to Mount Rigi. It was a day of intermittent sun and clouds, and I had no expectations of anything special. Arriving at Rigi, we took the cog railway about half way up, and then I set out to walk by myself. I was climbing around steep banks, covered with woods and pas-

---

[7] Plato, *Symposium.*

ture, listening to the sounds of cowbells around me, looking almost straight down to the lake far below. Patches of cloud and fog hung between me and glimpses of blue water. Somewhere out of all this surged the most intense excitement I had ever known, the thrill of discovering a new world. As I walked, ran, walked along the path, the lines of a poem kept running through my head:

Fear death? — to feel the fog in my throat,
   The mist in my face,
When the snows begin, and the blasts denote
   I am nearing the place....

I was ever a fighter, so — one fight more,
   The best and the last![8]

In fact I never was a fighter; up here I faced neither death nor struggle. Yet I was as though before something ultimate and wonderful, lifted up to something new. The past slipped away. Rejoining my parents, riding back down, getting aboard the boat, I continued inwardly as before. Standing on the foredeck of the boat as we returned under a grey sky, I felt my whole being opening in expectation. On the other side of the lake, facing green Rigi, was grey Mount Pilatus. As I looked at the long, steep meadows running up to its rocky sides, a place opened up in the clouds, and sunlight fell on the meadows, making the green shine brightly for a few moments. "If I could only be there, at that spot," I thought, as so many travelers in the mountains have thought before and since, "that would be heaven, true happiness. That is the place where I would receive everything."

[8]Robert Browning, "Prospice."

So we landed back at Lucerne, and everything continued as before, but by the end of that evening I knew with a deep certainty that someday I would become a priest. I observed the occasion by purchasing a missal at a store near the hotel and going to Mass the next morning. This was a view of my future which I had not had before, and now had. There had been a meeting. During the years that followed I often had occasion to wonder if I could really trust what I had then seen and felt. As it turned out, I could, and I did.

One more meeting. I have acted selfishly. I have betrayed a friend. I am ashamed of myself. Alone, in a hotel room, I look in a mirror. I see a stranger's face looking back at me, a face I never want to see again, and never have.

You will have better stories to tell, better because they are yours. I know people who, quite unexpectedly, have had more direct experiences of God than I ever have. One of our students stopped to pray in the church, and was unaccountably overwhelmed by a sense of God's nearness. He could not describe it, but the moment was one of beginning a new relationship. A friend of mine, a doctor who has never thought of himself as being very religious, lay down for an afternoon nap one day, and suddenly felt himself at the foot of an immense wall, a tremendous presence, which he knew beyond doubt to be God. These are the privileged, those who are surprised by direct grace. Had they been looking for it, they would not have found it. It is not our task to seek meeting in any form, but to examine the experiences we have, to see where meeting occurs. God was there all the time. "You would not be seeking me if you had not found me."[9] He was there,

9Blaise Pascal, *Pensées*.

but we were not. Yet, if we can now understand this, we can meet God in reflection on our experience, and so perhaps be readier the next time.

It seems, as one becomes older,
That the past has another pattern, and ceases to be a mere
    sequence—
Or even development: the latter a partial fallacy,
Encouraged by superficial notions of evolution,
Which becomes, in the popular mind, a means of disowning
    the past.
The moments of happiness — not the sense of well-being,
Fruition, fulfilment, security or affection,
Or even a very good dinner, but the sudden illumination—
We had the experience but missed the meaning,
And approach to the meaning restores the experience
In a different form, beyond any meaning
We can assign to happiness.[10]

Why should I speak of myself? Only for this reason — to encourage you to speak of yourself. My life presents nothing for you to look at. If I tell of experience with God, I speak only of inward events, things I cannot satisfactorily explain even to myself. What can be told is not the experience in question, because that experience cannot be told. What I have to say of myself is neither narrative nor explanation. What sort of discourse is left? I cannot ask you to look at me, nor to be me, but I can suggest that you stand beside me. You may not have felt or seen the things I have, but if you know the *sort* of thing I mean, you may be able to reflect on parallel incidents in your

---

[10]T. S. Eliot, *Four Quartets*, "The Dry Salvages."

own life. You can reflect for yourself, tell your own story. In this sense, there is no epiphany, there are just epiphanies.

This is the idea behind much of Sacred Scripture. To say that it contains revelation does not mean that it is a set of telegrams from God. Revelation consists in certain authors' accounts of their experience, experience whose meaning was that God was acting in those times and places in a very special way. "That which was from the beginning, which we have heard, which we have seen with our eyes, which we have looked upon and touched with our hands, concerning the word of life — the life was made manifest ['epiphanied'], and we saw it, and testify to it, and proclaim to you the eternal life which was with the Father and was made manifest to us." (1 Jn 1:1-2). When we read the text of a gospel, we hear the words of one who experienced Jesus. No matter how many different methods of analysis we bring to a text, treating it as a product of sources or a locus of influences, there remains a basic, unavoidable situation, that of witness: "He who saw it has borne witness — his testimony is true, and he knows that he tells the truth — that you also may believe" (Jn 19:35). That you also: we, like doubting Thomas, were not there when the events happened, at the foot of the cross or in the upper room. It is not enough for us to hear statements of fact. Like Thomas, we want to share the experience. Not seeing, we need nevertheless a means of encounter, a moment in which we can say, like Thomas, "My Lord and my God!" "That you also may believe." The gospel words are the story of those who encountered Jesus. Although this encounter is not ours, the story lets us stand beside those who speak. We cannot be Peter or John, but we can come to the fishing boat, or to the synagogue, or to Calvary as to the place of revelation. At this point the words of the gospel will be the occasion for *our own* encounter with the Lord. "That you also may believe" means that you also may have this encounter. Scripture is, as it were, the sacrament or catalyst, bringing me to a direct relationship with God. Because these are normative words, the canon of Scripture, I have confidence that it is really God whom I meet through them. I must constantly return to these words. Yet, when I have come to meet God at the moment of encounter, I no longer have the words. I experience something that happened before the gospel was written, and which still happens.

That is why each of us must tell his or her story. We must continue to witness, so that you may believe, although we know that our witness of itself will not bring about belief. If I speak of myself at the mountain, I do not ask you to look at the mountain or me, but at yourself. Perhaps you will look at a mountain of your own, the day you spent alone in a city, the time you talked with someone all night in a car and then, at dawn, said good-bye, or the afternoon it suddenly rained. You will remember how you felt once, when you heard a voice on the phone, or opened a letter, or went to a place you had never been and there made a decision. "Surely the Lord is in this place; and I did not know it" (Gen 28:16).

This is the end of the first cycle, the time of beginnings. It is the cycle of stirring and longing, of reaching up and reaching down. It is the time of birth and the time of doing humble tasks. It is the time of meeting, sudden understanding, the small moments of surprise which make all things new.

"Master, we toiled all night and took nothing! But at your word I will let down the nets." The greatest temptation is to suppose that there really is nothing new under the sun, that people never change, that there are no miracles. That is our world, not God's. It is we who, following our unlimited desires, have fashioned rigid orders of decency and death. Our social structures become ever more complicated as our desires grow and become ever more insatiable. "You desire and do not have; so you kill. And you covet and cannot obtain; so you fight and wage war. You do not have, because you do not ask. You ask and do not receive, because you ask wrongly, to spend it on your passions" (Ja 4:2-3).

If we believe that nothing can bend or change in the world of men, we have the religious option of flight. We may turn from all that is transitory, seeking escape in the infinite, happiness at the point of tranquillity. That, however, is not the way of Christ. If we are fleeing this world, we may pass Christ who is entering it. He takes flesh, this flesh in this fallen place. The first cycle is a pilgrimage which finds, after a necessary journey, the desired grace in the place where we began. The pilgrim's virtue is hope, holding fast to a possibility. After years of drinking and countless AA meetings, one day the alcoholic stops drinking. After years of clinging, the possessive parent lets go. After years of moves and counter-moves, a husband and wife listen to each other and understand. When they were least expecting it, after toiling all the night, all of a life, they let down the net just once more.

It is the cycle of new vision, which sees old things as though for the first time. "And he who sat upon the throne said, 'Behold! I make all things new'" (Rev 21:5). Even as the Savior's birth embraces our lowliness, so the final vision of salvation is that of a transformation of what is. A new light shines on that world which surrounds each of us, its all too familiar outlines. How much of it we avoid! From how many faces we turn away, scared of involvement or knowing that there is nothing we can do. Then, with epiphany, there is somewhere a change. We can reach out, and the word we speak, or the word we hear, makes a difference. What we desired was a shadow. What we got was a shape too gaunt to understand or love. At the end, there is another morning light.

> All for this, nature is never spent;
>> There lives the dearest freshness deep down things;
> And though the last lights off the black West went
>> Oh, morning, at the brown brink eastward springs —
> Because the Holy Ghost over the bent
>> World broods with warm breast and with ah! bright wings.[11]

[11]Gerard Manley Hopkins, "God's Grandeur."

II

THE CYCLE OF DEATH AND LIFE

4

The time of repentance: Lent

Therefore, behold, I will allure her,
    and bring her into the wilderness,
    and speak tenderly to her (Hos 2:14).

The second cycle moves to a deeper level. If the first is poetic, the cycle of meeting and new understanding, the second is dramatic, the cycle of suffering and new life.

The starting point of the first was desire, expansion of the self. Now the starting point is guilt, the sense of our diminishment. As sinners we rise first, then fall. As a redeemer, God continues ever downward until he can pick us up. We begin from where we are, first examining our desires, and now our sense of sin.

It is the work of the Holy Spirit to convince the world of sin. I can't think of a more difficult task, although Jesus had made it his own in the first words of his mission: "The time is fulfilled, and the kingdom of God is at hand; repent, and believe in the gospel" (Mk 1:15). The baptist, clearing a way for this message, had to draw people out of their towns, and into the desert. Repentance was too dramatic to be undertaken at home. How difficult must it be to preach repentance today?

Original sin is a nearly forgotten doctrine. It is a largely unquestioned assumption of our culture that guilt is but a psychological misfortune from which an enlightened education or, if necessary, treatment can deliver innocent sufferers. Secularism has created a myth of innocence, to replace what it sees as an old myth of guilt. It sees the moral codes of the recent past as excessively burdensome and restricting, and nowhere more so than in conservative religious milieux where God, clergymen, and parents all conspired to oppress the growing child. The sinister priest, "the man who invented sin," was the stock figure in the mythology, the man who imposed guilt on others as a form of social control. Because it did not believe in the inherent goodness of the person, but rather in his sinfulness, the old myth was seen to trade liberty for outward order, self-fulfillment for self-control.

The counter claims of the secularist myth resemble those which, in the fifth century, the Pelagians advanced against traditional Christians. Man is seen as naturally good and capable, through his unaided ethical efforts, of working out his own salvation. The thing to notice about this Pelagianism, though, is that it is not someone else's view. It is ours, and we have used it for some of our most enlightened reforms. Education was once thought of as a process of correction, but now of development and growth. To state it as baldly as that is to see to what extent the secularist view is a part of our thinking. Who wants to return to the Puritan severities of the birch rod? Who would dare deny the progress education has made toward a healthier view of children? There is a danger of inconsistency for those who lament the excesses of permissive child raising and progressive education, given that those critics probably share to a fair degree in the philosophy which underlies the things they criticize. As a teacher, I am often amazed at the way parents worry about the bad influences of other children on their children, but never about the bad influences of their children on other children. Why not face the fact that we're all in this permissive thing together, the children included?

If secularism is to do away with the concept of guilt, it must — and does — shy away from moral absolutes. Instead of the old commandments, "thou shalt" and "thou shalt not," society prefers to impose the more modest expectations of behavioral adjustment, good self-image, and successful role-playing. The individual seeks comfort, acceptance from others, to be OK. Starting from a view of man's basic innocence and of his quest for self-fulfillment in society, this modern Pelagianism arrives at a doctrine of self-justification.

If secularism would really silence the stern voice of the commandments, and if the voice came from a law-giving God, that God had to die. This, of course, was seen to by Nietzsche and others, and today it is no secret that the philosophy of guiltlessness is also the philosophy of atheism. It is an irony in recent intellectual history that a brace of theologians, in their zeal to restore to man all his rights and privileges, have been among the loudest partisans of this philosophy. It amounts to this: you can do what you want because, ultimately, there is no-one to tell you not to. Your salvation is what you make of yourself.

While there is a certain euphoria to be experienced in a conversion to this view, it is, as many college freshmen discover, short-lived. Spontaneity is replaced by anxiety.

Granted that I can do anything, what in fact should I do? That all things would be permitted if God did not exist was a prospect which seriously alarmed Dostoievsky, who foresaw the moral chaos in which we now live.[1] In this century it alarmed Camus as well, when he argued in *The Rebel* that, since God does not exist, we must be even stricter with ourselves than a God would have been.[2] It has not worked out that way. Few atheist secularists share Camus' high seriousness, according to which we shoulder the burden for all our ethical choices. While some become their own taskmasters and lawgivers, more prefer to enjoy life now and pay later. In an age of loose personal morals and rising consumption, waste, and violence, as the incidence of divorce and alcoholism continues to climb, I am waiting for somebody to undertake a proof that, with the cult of permissiveness, we are all truly freer and happier.

The worst part of secularist culture is that it is unhealthy and tragic not to have any moral absolutes, and not to be able to admit guilt when we have sinned. In a brilliant study of the philosophical implications of Freud, Lionel Trilling traces the death of God movement as part of man's assertion of his radical authenticity, of his being as undetermined from without.[3] He goes on to note the devastating psychological effects that this position has had on those who hold it. With the absence of God there is an absence of any fixed standard by which we can measure ourselves or even find our ethical beargins. It is a sense of no limits and no check-points, no landmarks; it is free floating in a viscous goo, feeling no reason

[1] See *The Brothers Karamazov*, XI.9.

[2] Albert Camus, *The Rebel*, II.

[3] Lionel Trilling, *Sincerity and Authenticity* (Cambridge, Mass.: Harvard, 1972), ch. 6.

why we should do one thing rather than another. Trilling relates this loss of sign posts to the demise of narrative literature, the loss of our sense of the past. Nothing is given; we have only ourselves.

Seen in this way, guilt may be healthier than the absence of guilt. Trilling thinks that Freud moved toward this conclusion as he grew older. In his earlier writings he saw neuroses as caused by hidden repressions, and represseions as having been caused by social strictures. Later in *Civilisation and Its Discontents*, Freud rejected the earlier, more facile view. If society is the cause of our moral suffering, who is responsible for society being as it is? Surely men make society before society makes men. In fact, Freud now speaks at length of the super-ego, a repressing and self-persecuting part of the psyche which is just as deeply rooted and inaccessible to rational control as the law-breaking id. Freud, then, moves from the conventional liberal notion of guilt as imposed on us by the agents of social control to the starker reality of guilt as imposed on us by ourselves. Freud was led to confess that man's guilt, and hence his sense of suffering, are probably irremediable, and Trilling suggests that such a conclusion may be the necessary price to pay if we are to avoid lives totally devoid of meaning. The image of the painfully dying Freud, outraged at the well-meaning doctor who had given him a sedative and demanding *by what right* this had been done, is symbolic of the moralist's insistence on the sense of reality which could only be achieved through the experience, however painful, of limits.

Freud, of course, remained an atheist, leaving Trilling and others to speculate on the extent to which the severe and self-punishing super-ego resembles the law-giving God which Freud had so long ago abandoned. If there is no God, anything is permitted. If anything is permitted, there is no human accountability and a state of sickness worse than the anxieties of guilt. .

A more recent psychiatrist, Karl Menninger, has developed the point in his *Whatever Became of Sin?* People bear their guilt because they cannot admit it. Their value systems provide no place where such burdens may be laid down. Secular atheism set out to free men from an old tyranny by slaying the tyrant. Can secular atheism now admit that man lives in a worse tyranny, a slave to himself? Their achievement was not to kill God, but only to destroy many people's faith in the real God who is steadfast in mercy and loving-kindness, who alone is powerful to forgive and remove the guilt which man alone incurs.

A further unpleasant result of the death of God is the death of the other things God gave us, such as human love. The theatre of sexuality is a good place to watch the drama of unhappy freedom. Is it accurate, today, to speak of a sexual revolution? Sexual desire and licentiousness have always been with us. The only new thing is the universal removal of restraints. Disapproving voices in church and society have grown quieter: there are fewer condemnations of divorce, fornication, or homosexuality. There is indeed no-one to say no. Young people are genuinely surprised to hear me advise them against pre-marital sex on moral grounds, and sceptical when they hear that it falls within the scope of the sixth commandment. If everyone is doing it, if it is simply part of a young person's milieu, what kind of sense does it make for me to say that it is wrong? I must sound to them like a priest telling people that it is immoral to do gardening Sunday.

Does this mean that there are no more commandments,

and therefore no more sin? My students would certainly not go this far, but they are just as certainly uncomfortable with principles imposed on them from an absolute source. They would far rather replace those with their own maxims, like the shopworn "as long as it doesn't hurt others." They do not yet realize that this is only the beginning of new difficulties. If my ethical principles are not from God but from myself, are they absolute, or can I change them? How do I know if I have the right ones? What is to prevent me from breaking my own principles, and what do I do when I have broken them? Camus' Clamence had an iron clad rule never to sleep with the wives of his friends. Shortly before he slept with such women, their husbands ceased to be his friends. [4]

The young Catholics I know, as they are growing up, must perform philosophical exercises for themselves. Like Clamence, they often rationalize and justify their conduct, even if implicitly, in order to avoid the experience of sin and guilt. Since they do not see their situation in terms of commandments and transgression, it does little good for me to impress these concepts on them. There is, however, another way to approach the matter.

When a young person first has intercourse — say, as a teenager — it may be for a variety of reasons, none of which he has clearly formulated to himself. He is curious, he wants to be a man, he feels that he is at the stage in a relationship where this is appropriate, or he just wants fun and pleasure. Life has something to offer him, and he takes it.

I am talking to him, and I suggest that what he is doing is basically selfish. He disagrees. He does it only with his girl-

[4]Camus, *The Fall*, ch. 3.

friend, and feels strongly about her. He cares about her, does not take advantage of her. What's wrong with that? Just the fact that some old people say it's wrong? Even though I recognize that he and his girlfriend give a great deal to each other, I still say that his sexual conduct is essentially a matter of taking. It is eros, an expression of passion for a highly desirable good, some good which the lover does not yet possess. Whether the good be physical, spiritual, or a combination of the two, it is the lover who seeks this good from the beloved, and for himself. Tristan gives his life for the prize of Isolde, whereas the lecher gives only a sum of money for a prostitute. In both cases, however, the lover gives what he gives so that he may attain a good for himself. Even if Tristan worships Isolde, becomes her slave, it is all in exchange for that good of love which he seeks.

The love of generous giving, agape, is different. Eros desires for itself a good which it does not yet possess, a good which it perceives in the beloved. It is that desire which, in Advent, we saw reaching ever higher. Agape is God's stooping down. It desires no good for itself, and its love is not inspired by a good perceived in the beloved. The model for agape is God's love for us. There is little in us to attract God to desire something which he lacks. It is rather God who freely bestows on us what we lack. God's agape expresses itself to us in a covenant, a commitment wherein God gives us life and redemption without regard for what we give him. All we need to do is be faithful to the covenant — a hard enough task.

Why has God given us sexuality? What part does it play in his plan for us? Silly question? "Reproduction," we answer, and then add, "and for love." And what do we mean by love? Do we mean eros, the constant striving to satisfy desire? We then reflect that marriages based solely on eros burn intensely and then die, as desire turns elsewhere. A lifetime commitment between husband and wife needs a great deal more than eros. Not that sexual passion is wrong; it is a vital part of sexual relationships. Still, it is not everything. The fallacious equation of "love" with "romantic love" (or eros) leads to the classic double standard, where sexuality is divided into two compartments. One is reproduction: the wife. The other is love: the mistress. It has been suggested, and I think with some cogency, that the position of the Catholic Church on birth control has reflected the fact that it has long condoned, at least implicitly, this double standard among its own Latin people.[5] There is a much closer connection between reproduction and love. The act of sex is a gift of life, that is, it is the act by which two people give their lives to each other. That is the essential thing. A man and woman leave their families and cleave to each other; they become one flesh. They give themselves away. St. Paul takes this idea so literally as to see in the act of sex a metaphysical giving-away of the self, whether intended or not: "Do you not know that he who joins himself to a prostitute becomes one body with her? For, as it is written, 'The two shall become one'" (1 Cor 6:16). The appropriate relationship for such self-gift is marriage, and the event of procreation is the

---

[5]Janusz Korczak (who is responsible for "the year of the child," and who was a non-religious Jew until quite late in his life), while waiting with the children of his orphanage to be sent to their deaths in the gas chambers, wrote in his diary: ". . . most intimately connected with death are sterilization, and the prevention and interruption of pregnancy." One may ask if Korczak, sitting with his children in what has been called the kingdom of death, saw more deeply into the truth of traditional Judaeo-Christian ethical teachings than we, its exponents, who are living the life of this world and share, however unwittingly, its point of view. (Note contributed by Abbot Matthew Stark.)

possibility within that relationship which is both the symbol and the effect of this kind of love. Two people give their lives to each other, and the result of that gift is a new life. The fact that a man and a woman are open to the creation of new life at some point in their relationship is the seal on their gift, the bond that keeps them in responsibility to each other and to their child. The morality of sex, for them as for my teenagers, comes to this question: are they seeking a good (passion) for themselves, or are they giving a good (themselves) to each other?

The boy whom I have gently accused of selfishness cares for his girlfriend, and she for him, but this caring has its limits. They are not giving their lives to each other, and they certainly are not open to the creation of a new life. Is their intercourse sinful? Yes. But why? The act is not a bad thing in itself, and can it not be seen as what is appropriate to what these two people feel about each other at the time? Some day will not they, or two other people, in fact be making this gift? That, I think, is not so certain. Our young man or woman begins to have intercourse sometime as a teenager, and eventually marries, let us say ten years later. What happens during this time? A regular indulgence in sex, a regular satisfaction of passion. Perhaps there are long-term relationships, perhaps there are one-night stands, and perhaps there is a great deal in between. It doesn't matter. The point is not the morality of any one sexual act, but rather what is implied by the whole of that person's sexual activity. After ten years of eros, of basically self-centered love, how successfully can our young people convert to agape, to generous giving? After a certain age, says Clamence, every man is responsible for the look on his face. The habit of self-seeking in love is not easily broken. It is passion, very strong passion, and it forges very strong chains around the ego. In a time of increasing sexual permissiveness in youth, we are naive to be shocked at the spiraling divorce rates. If love is indeed to be a part of marriage, even to *be* marriage, and if we also want the marriage to last, we will have to find a better idea of love than the eros we know so well.

My young friend does not want to be called a "fornicator," nor to be told that what he is doing is sinful. It sounds, he says, like an outmoded idea, as though you call bad something which is good. The point is not that sex is bad, but that it is indeed good, much better than these teenagers imagine. They are using it in a way which makes them blind to the real good for which these acts were intended. They may be using one of the greatest means we have of imitating God, of giving ourselves to others, of displacing our personal center, for aggrandizing the self and taking from others. It is dangerous here to generalize about all sexual activity, and impossible to evaluate how much giving and taking there is between individuals. I do not judge, but ask others to judge themselves, and honestly to ask in what direction their morality is moving. This boy or girl, candidly well intentioned and without scruples or self-criticism, needs to be warned of the danger of an ever growing egotism. The problem lies less in the idea that he or she is committing sins than in the fact that they are entering further and further into a state of sinfulness.

The death of God and the banishment of guilt were to have emancipated man but, as in the case of other revolutions, poor man has ended up more of a slave than before. Man is the measure of all things, said Protagoras, but Socrates asked what, if this be so, is the measure of man? That is still our dilemma. If there is no God, and if anything is permitted, then how can I measure my actions, myself? If I am the measure of all things, must I so distort the world as to curve it all around the center of myself? And will each person try to curve the same reality around each separate self? It was St. Teresa of Avila's vision of hell that the lost souls now wanted to love God but, by the implicit decision of their self-centered lives, were no longer capable of doing so. They sent out impulses of love to God which fatally returned to them negatively, as a burning, a frustrated love which consumes itself.[6] It is the final outcome of the perversion of giving to another as taking for oneself: total preoccupation with self.

> Selfyeast of spirit a dull dough sours. I see
> The lost are like this, and their scourge to be
> As I am mine, their sweating selves; but worse.[7]

It would, however, be inaccurate to say that the banishment of guilt is only the work of atheists. How many times have we heard that the God of the Old Testament is the God of law and justice, but that the God of the New Testament is the God of mercy and love? Reviving the ancient Marcionite heresy, too many Christians today reject large parts of Scripture in order to fashion their own God of love. They seem to paraphrase Augustine's *ama et fac quod vis* to mean, "It doesn't matter what you do as long as you're sincere." Such an appropriation of the gospel without the law tends to change the gospel into the exact opposite of what it is, a charter for self-indulgence instead of a call to radical displacement of the self in favor of God and my neighbor.

[6]Teresa of Avila, *Autobiography*, 32, as interpreted in *The Sermons and Devotional Writings of Gerard Manley Hopkins* (London: Oxford, 1959), pp. 136-138; see also Hopkins' poem, "I cast for comfort."

[7]Hopkins, "I wake and feel the fell of dark, not day."

The uncompromising voice of the commandments, being *another's* voice, stands in radical opposition to the self as a moral standard. It was the sin of Adam and Eve to substitute human criteria for divine, to replace God as the standard or center of their actions. The decalogue is a constant reminder that man is not the measure of all things. As such, it is the basis of Jesus' teachings: "Think not that I have come to abolish the law and the prophets: I have come not to abolish them but to fulfill them" (Mk 5:17). Once the law has established otherness in terms of obedience to God and justice to others, Jesus then fulfills it, transposing it into terms of love of God and neighbor. "Otherness" is the indispensable constant. Without it, we will be tempted to take Jesus' words as a sentimental "ethic of love," transposing them into what we think of as love: romantic self-centeredness. This is precisely the attitude, as old as Adam and Eve, from which the law, the prophets, and Jesus are trying to save us.

If even the words of Jesus come to us through a filter of our self-centered presuppositions, how is it possible to hear the gospel any more? This is the function of the forty days: to leave our accustomed bases, to go to the desert, to see and hear afresh. Everything in us will resist setting out on the second cycle, because it is a new and strange world, one which threatens to take away the personal supports we cling to most tightly. The beginning of the second cycle is the call to an alteration of our perspective. We have spent so much of our lives learning to perform successfully, to impress people, to gain status, to be admitted by committees of selection, to win arguments, to have good self concepts. Now none of that matters. Not in the desert, not during the forty days. Now, we are being called to repentance.

What does it mean to repent? The Greek word, *metanoia*, means a change of mind, a sudden alteration of point of view. In the previous chapter I mentioned a disagreeable moment of seeing a strange face in the mirror. That was a moment of *metanoia*, a sudden perception of myself as sinful, perhaps as I really was just then, followed by a powerful desire to change. Insight and sorrow, leading to joy. The moment of repentance is a moment of grace. David is insensitive to the sin he has committed with, and then against, Bathsheba until the prophet Nathan tells him the parable about the rich man taking away the poor man's one sheep. When David indignantly says that the rich man should be killed, Nathan inserts the knife: "Thou art the man" (2 Sam 12:7). Peter, after protesting his unswerving loyalty to Jesus, and being told that he will betray the Lord before the cock crows, hears the cock, and sees all. He weeps bitterly (Lk 22:62). Peter, again, mindful of what he learned, is now preaching to the Jews after the Ascension. After a long explanation of who the real Messiah is, he turns on his hearers: " 'Let all the house of Israel therefore know assuredly that God has made him both Lord and Christ, this Jesus whom you crucified.' Now when they heard this, they were cut to the heart, and said to Peter and the rest of the apostles, 'Brethren, what shall we do?' And Peter said to them, 'Repent, and be baptized . . .' " (Ac 2:37-38).

Note that in each case the hearer is shocked, cut to the heart. The technical term for this is compunction, a piercing stab which enters the heart, often lancing it of the infection of some sin and purifying it for contact with God. If, as so often happens, we are kept away from God by the hardness of our hearts, the moment of compunction is itself the moment of encounter, the moment of self-revelation and of God's revelation to us.

Sometimes sudden awareness of ourselves is a dangerous thing. While Peter was weeping, Judas was hanging himself. "Godly grief produces a repentance that leads to salvation and brings no regret, but worldly grief produces death" (2 Cor 7:10). We are summoned to awake, but would some be better off left sleeping? We all know some sleeping dogs that we ourselves are not going to disturb, and perhaps we wonder if we are the same, if others have decided to let us be. Perhaps, indeed, we would all be deranged by an undisguised view of all there is in our unconscious personality. The gospel does not threaten us with the horror of our naked selves, just as it does not bring us face to face with God. It asks us only to forego the self-deception of those who suppose that they can do without God. The emperor need not look in the mirror, but he should heed the one candid child.

True compunction, as opposed to self-analysis, may begin with an uneasy feeling that something is not right, something for which there is no remedy to be purchased. In T. S. Eliot's *The Cocktail Party*, Celia's conversion begins with a sense of sin.

REILLY.   You suffer from a sense of sin, Miss Coplestone? This is
             most unusual.
                         CELIA. It seemed to me abnormal.

She has no way of accounting for the origin of this idea.

CELIA.   Well, my bringing up was pretty conventional —
            I had always been taught to disbelieve in sin.

> Oh, I don't mean that it was ever mentioned!
> But anything wrong, from our point of view,
> Was either bad form, or was psychological.

She finally says how she feels.

> It's not the feeling of anything I've ever *done*,
> Which I might get away from, or of anything in me
> I could get rid of — but of emptiness, of failure
> Towards someone, or something, outside of myself;
> And I feel I must . . . *atone* — is that the word?
> Can you treat a patient for such a state of mind?[8]

This is the moment at which Celia begins to turn from a secular and empty life to one of heroic sanctity, ending in martyrdom.

Albert Camus' *The Fall* is an expression of non-Christian compunction. The hero is a prophet, Jean-Baptiste Clamence (John Baptist *clamans*), with no message and nowhere to point, "an empty prophet for bad times, Elijah with no Messiah." At first a successful lawyer, a man of vaulting ego and self-nourishing virtues, he had suddenly begun to discover cracks in his edifice. His refusal to save a woman from drowning reveals to him his unwillingness to do good except on his own terms. With that the fall began, and continued until Clamence ended in a dive in Amsterdam, a city whose concentric circles suggest those of Dante's hell, buying drinks for strangers to whom he confesses his sins in the hope of

[8]T. S. Eliot, *The Cocktail Party. The Complete Poems and Plays, 1909-1950* (N.Y.: Harcourt, Brace and World, 1971), pp. 361-362. This theme is also treated in my introduction to I. Hausherr, *Penthos* (Kalamazoo, Mich.: Cistercian Publications, 1982).

leading them to do the same — a judge-penitent. The unrelenting Clamence depicts us as maintaining our own innocence only by fastening guilt on others. Violence is the last resort of our own quest for self-justification. The pathos of it all is that, for the atheist Camus, there is no source of forgiveness. A beggar had once grasped his hand and said, "Ah, monsieur, it is not that one is bad, but one loses the light." "Yes," adds Clamence, "we have lost the light, the mornings, the holy innocence of him who forgives himself."[9] At the end, we leave Clamence supplicating an empty sky and spinning further ironies about his situation.

Like Clamence, the Christian begins his repentance by abandoning his claims of independent virtue. In this sense, the sinner is indeed closer to grace than the pharisee who thanks God that he is not like the rest of men. Unlike Clamence, however, the one who repents is not cynical about himself. Neither is he scrupulous, nor a despiser of God's creation. Repentance should be produced, as should any moment of grace, by a sudden awareness of the self in the presence of God. On the night that Jesus worked the miraculous catch of fish, Peter fell at his feet crying, "Depart from me, Lord, for I am a sinful man" (Lk 5:8). Isaiah, introduced to a vision of the divine splendor, cried, "Woe is me! For I am lost; for I am a man of unclean lips . . ." (Is 6:5). The appearance of God, his presence, is a fire which burns away the dross of all that is near it. What is perfect points, by its very being, to what is imperfect. The one who comes to save sinners must, by the nature of his task, first convince sinners that they need to be saved. Under the cross we stand convicted: the pharisee of

[9]Camus, *The Fall*, ch. 6.

self-righteousness, the lover of self-seeking, the parent of possessiveness, the child of ingratitude, all of us of self-centeredness. Unless we agree to stand so convicted, there can be no salvation for us. We are asked neither to condemn ourselves nor to think of ourselves hypocritcally as worse than others. We are asked only to abandon our claims to self-righteousness and so to accept the new center. To be justified is to accept God's justice instead of our own, and that, precisely, is repentance.

There are many ways of turning:

> Whether at once, as once at a crash Paul,
> Or as Austin, a lingering-out sweet skill . . . [10]

There are some Pauls, but most of us are Augustines, for whom repentance is a life-long pilgrimage. There are moments of compunction all along the way; had we but eyes, we would find more than enough to get us to heaven. Our lives provide a generous share of frustrations, embarrassments, disappointments. Our worldly reaction to this is just the opposite of what it should be. The wound is inflicted, but instead of allowing it to open us with softening and healing, we absorb it, cover it, and grow calluses around the sore spot. Having been wounded, we grow harder, more closed.

As we grow older and look back, the chances for repentance increase. We have regrets. Will these be the occasion of hardening or softening, of closing or opening of the heart? How shall we look on the opportunities missed, the false paths followed to a dead end, the incomplete friendships, the tasks unfinished, the time wasted?

[10]Hopkins, "The Wreck of the Deutschland."

Having shed one mask, we must then shed the next one. You get converted from intellectual pride to a life of caring for others. Then you have to be converted from possessiveness, the need to be needed, to something else. I don't think I know what that is; I haven't arrived there yet. The sequence differs, and there are so many masks. The mask of Martha and the mask of Mary, the mask of the profligate and the mask of the prude, the robust mask and the sensitive mask. You keep peeling them off. I think the Oriental belief is that, after everything is taken away, there is nothing left; it was all illusion, ending in a joke, an absurdity. There was no onion after all. The Christian belief is different. There really is a core of our personality, something called "heart" or "soul." Each acceptance of healing compunction, each effort of repentance, brings us just a little closer to the reality of that place where we meet God face to face. It's a long path, but it's worth it.

"If today you would hear his voice. . . ." The cock crows. One who passes amid soldiers gives me a quiet look of love, and suddenly I realize that I care more for myself than for him, than for anyone. I weep, not so much from any self-revulsion as from disappointment. I said I would be faithful, but it was too much. I wish I could love, strongly and faithfully. Why can't I be the person I want to be, the person I say I will be? I feel no better than Judas. Is this what I *am*? Cowardly, impulsive, loud, unreliable? I would never admit that, but when the Lord is near, all those defenses dissolve. Depart from me, Lord, for I am, I really am, a sinful man.

Lent calls us to the desert, a place we rarely visit. It is a place where the Lord will pass; a place where we are exposed to him. There is no hiding, just barren reality. No masks. "If today you would hear his voice, do not harden your hearts, as in the wilderness" (Ps 95:8). The issue of repentance comes to this: shall we go to the desert? Can we bear to lose in a short time what it has taken us so long to acquire? Can we bear to admit what we have been so long in denying? Can we bear to let go? To relinquish ourselves as center? To stand before God as sinful so that we may be saved, to know sorrow so that we may know joy?

In the first cycle, the gift of God responded to our desire; now it responds to our need. First we reached out in confidence to the expected good. Now we withdraw in hope from the illusory good. First we sought visions and gifts. Now we seek healing and a new start.

To repent is to learn. We have learned to deny our past while accepting its total outcome in the present. Both the denial and the acceptance are made possible through forgiveness, a denial of what is not and an acceptance of what is. We propose and ask to do God's will, not ours, and so to continue in what is, rather than in illusion. Yet we find ourselves going back again and again to the old shadows. Yet again we turn, and in receiving forgiveness we get reality back once again. Every evening we begin our office of Compline with the words, "Turn us, O God our saviour." Every evening it needs to be said anew.

It often feels like the labor of Sisyphus: up and down, up and down. In fact, though, each exchange of repentance and mercy is a step forward into the center itself, into the mystery of all reality. Each mask removed is a step to the heart, to the place where Jesus dies and lives again.

5

Time at the center: Easter

In saying, "He ascended," what does it mean but that he had also descended into the lower parts of the earth? He who descended is he who also ascended far above all the heavens, that he might fill all things (Eph 4:9-10).

Why should I be alive? Until we can answer this question, says Camus at the beginning of *The Myth of Sisyphus*, all other philosophical questions should wait their turn.

Sometimes the stage sets collapse. Rising, streetcar, four hours in the office or the factory, meal, streetcar, four hours of work, meal, sleep, and Monday Tuesday Wednesday Thursday Friday and Saturday according to the same rhythm — this path is easily followed most of the time. But one day the "why" arises and everything begins in that weariness tinged with amazement.[1]

[1]Camus, *The Myth of Sisyphus* (N.Y.: Vintage, 1955), p. 10.

I think that most of the moral and spiritual problems our students have come back to the question of life and death. Is there any other purpose to life than just doing certain things day after day? Colleges and schools are just beginning to acknowledge and deal with the problem of suicide; until recently they just pretended it wasn't there. Who on a large campus is responsible for a lonely young person in despair? Who can detect the inner tearing of a boy being pulled to pieces by the conflicts of a driving ambition and an engulfing hedonism? Who can convince a lonely and depressed girl that her existence is important to others?

Our culture attempts to absorb life and death into its technology. We use abortion to kill the children we have and don't want, and are developing ways to synthesize the children we don't have and, presumably, want. We have techniques for keeping people alive after their rendez-vous with death, and now we are getting legal procedures for deciding when the rendez-vous will, after all, take place. We also have techniques for ending life ahead of schedule. We pay our funeral directors to disguise death, but for all these efforts there is no controlling it.

Death, in fact, stalks our century as it never has before. Let us say that, since 1900, one hundred million people have died as a result of warfare and political violence. Is that an accurate estimate? What does it matter? Can you conceive of 10,000,000 murdered people with greater peace of mind than 100,000,000 murdered people? Men, women, and children shot, burned, impaled, drowned, tortured, hanged, or bludgeoned — stockpiles of corpses. Put them together in a Gehenna of today: one stockpile of one hundred million murdered bodies. We cannot even conceive of this reality in coherent terms. The figures are too great, and we have seen too many images in photographs and newsreels. Too many distended bodies of starving children, too many pistols fired at point blank, too many faces of men about to die. Can we conceive of just one, one single person enduring torture and death?

I once made the mistake of taking *Doctor Zhivago* to the dentist's office. Reading as I waited for a wisdom tooth to be extracted, I came to the passage where a soldier is brought in, having received a piece of shrapnel which cut straight through his jaw and lodged there. Someone tries to take the shrapnel out. Screaming, the man dies. This scene, followed by my experience of the extraction of one wisdom tooth, made me an emotional pacifist for a year or two after that. What would it have been like to get that drill without novocaine? What is physical pain? What is shrapnel, slicing all the nerves in all my teeth? What is third degree burning over all my body? What is torture? How can I multiply that, conceive it in six figures, in nine figures? I cannot conceive of it, and so I don't. The newsreels show me enough horror to render me quite insensitive to the whole thing. It is a moral vaccine. We take a little of the poison on the six o'clock news, and we stay immune.

Besides, those things don't happen here. Portsmouth, Rhode Island, now that summer has come, is covered with a gentle green; this monastery and school is a haven of peace. All around us, Middle America goes to work and play, wasteful and profligate perhaps, but trying to maintain some decency. It can't happen here. I walk in our woods and come to the creek. Its name is Bloody Run, so named after the revolutionary battle fought here in August, 1778, when the water ran red. You can find chips of gravestones in the grass around the pond. During the Civil War they put up a military hospital just to the south of us, near Melville. The worst cases were there, and since they had no sterilization and no anaesthesia, the screams from that building could be heard around the clock. This too I can neither picture nor understand in this place of peace, today.

Yet I, as a priest, must understand life and death, and give some answers to others who so badly want to know. Is there a life after death? Really? How do you know? Does it make any difference how I live now? Does my life now have any ultimate significance? What is really important to me? Of what importance am I to others? What do I really know about any of this?

My Christian religion is a matter of life and death. These are its realities, not pious myths. The Incarnation was a real birth. The Crucifixion was a real death. Although I don't understand how these things could happen to God, I believe that they did indeed happen, and that they happened to God. Then there is Resurrection. As for birth and death, at least I know what these are, but Resurrection is of itself a mystery. Still, I believe that this, too, really happened.

"If Christ is not risen," says Saint Paul, "our faith is in vain; and we are found to be the most miserable of men" (1 Cor 15:17). There are biblical scholars who chide those of us who believe in the Resurrection as a "mere" historical event. Historical facts are known, but the Resurrection can only be believed. Hence, runs the argument, the Resurrection cannot be considered an historical event at all. On this account the Resurrection seems like the tree in the forest — in this case it has to be believed in order to be there. From there we go to spiritual talk of the new man and risenness, but we hear little of the rising of Jesus as something that really happened.

Either it did or it didn't. No-one saw Jesus rise from the dead. They saw him die, and be buried, and they saw the empty tomb, and finally they saw him alive, and to all of this they gave witness. What happened on the morning after the sabbath is not a matter of metaphor or myth. The disciples in the upper room, and those on the road to Emmaus, did not just have experiences of new existence. They saw Jesus, who had been dead and was alive. Their account is either true or false, and is offered to our belief as it has been offered to the belief of all Christians from then to now. If it did not really happen, there is nothing to believe.

Why do we find belief in the Resurrection so difficult? There are two reasons. First, we trivialize Jesus' sufferings. We are docetists who have seen too many pious crucifixes and absorbed too much religious sentimentality to appreciate the stark human reality of Jesus. We think of him as a sugary superman, somehow incapable of real suffering. I ask the boys what the Crucifixion was all about, and they answer dutifully that it is God "showing us his love," as though the Passion were a passion play. I once heard a religion teacher refer to the cross as the greatest of all visual aids, and I'm afraid that he was not joking.

On the other hand, if someone rubs our nose in the mystery, and shows us a dead body in a grave, still there after thirty-six hours, we think and say that dead bodies just don't rise from the dead. We use our scientific view of things as a yardstick to measure the gospel message, consigning to myth whatever will not meet our specifications. Besides, there is Frazier's *Golden Bough*, with all that mythological business about the dying and rising god. And yet, and yet — the New

Testament itself and the witness of the Church from Easter day until now continue to testify to that one event whereby Jesus is Lord. Either it happened or it didn't happen. If it didn't happen, then our faith is in vain, there is no salvation, there is nothing to reinterpret, and we are the most miserable of men.

If it really did happen, what was it all about? Why did Jesus have to die? What direct effect does that death have on me? I have always been perplexed to find that this mystery, the crucial one in the story of our redemption, should be so embarrassingly difficult to explain. "This is it!" I have often told my religion class, secretly hoping that they would not ask me why.

Not that there is any lack of explanations. The Latin tradition, as in Anselm's *Cur Deus Homo*, sees an offended God and a humanity hopelessly in debt, a debt which could only have been paid off by the Son. A later version of this view pictured an angry God, whose wrath against man could only be assuaged by the blood of Christ. The underlying picture of God as an exactor of retribution makes the redemption implausible as a work of God himself. God so loved the world? Furthermore, the death of Jesus in this theory appears only as a juridical procedure, not something which really changes man's being. A contrary view — Gustaf Aulén calls it the "classical" theory — sees the whole work of redemption as God acting for us.[2] What God does, through the death and Resurrection of his son, is to engage in an ultimate struggle with evil, the prize being possession of the world. Each side

[2]Gustaf Aulén, *Christus Victor* (N.Y.: Macmillan, 1969).

has used its last weapon: evil has brought forth death and God has brought forth new life out of death. Whereas the first view saw God as an exacting master, the second sees him as coming to free us from the real tyrant, the devil. God was in Christ and is at work even in us who believe, reconciling us *to himself* (cf. 2 Cor 5:19).

While this second view gives a more satisfactory account of the relationship between God and his redeemed, it runs into the problem of dualism. Does this idea of combat suggest that the power of evil was primordial, an absolute adversary of God? Although the classical proponents of the doctrine would deny that, their view still seems to approach the two-god universe, a place of essential conflict. Augustine, whose account of Manicheaism in his *Confessions* is a primer of dualism, shows the dualist picture of man as a battlefield over which two contenders are struggling for the prize of his soul.[3] While the classic doctrine of atonement sees man as definitively redeemed, dualism tends to see unending renewal of this struggle, an *agon* to which man must repeatedly and passively submit himself.

The one thing which both "Latin" and "classical" theories have in common is that Jesus, on their account, redeems us by satisfying some condition extrinsic to human nature. To redeem means to "buy back," and both theories see Jesus' death as the price for man exacted either by an otherwise insuperable devil or by an otherwise implacable God. In both cases there is a cosmic division over man: either a merciful Son satisfying an exacting Father, or both Father and Son pitted

[3]See Peter Brown, *Augustine of Hippo* (London: Faber and Faber, 1967), pp. 46-60.

against the Adversary. Both theories fail to give enough emphasis to evil as within man, to redemption as saving man from himself.

Perhaps this is just what Irenaeus, the great proponent of the "classical" view, meant in such phrases as these: "The Word of God . . . overcoming the devil through man"; "mankind, that had fallen into captivity, is now by God's mercy delivered out of the power that had held them in bondage."[4] I certainly do not mean to make light of the devil. The trouble with even the word "devil," at least in present day American English, is that its connotations tend to make trivialities of evil and sin. As our culture has developed a taste for super-terrestrial sensationalism, the devil has come into fashion. The alien force, the "thing," the attacker from the outside, is always good box-office. The current stream of diabolic novels and films, in order to titillate, portrays the devil in such grotesque forms as to reduce his credibility to a vanishing point. The more scary he gets, the more deliciously unreal. Some portrayals, notably C. S. Lewis' *Screwtape Letters*, have tried to make us take the devil seriously, but what are a few enlightened books against a whole mass culture?

The devil is the Prince of this world; hence, to be satanic is to be worldly, which includes being eminently respectable. The devil is no actor in an x-rated film. He shares our humdrum lives and inspires their vices. Dubious business dealings, gossip, conspicuous consumption and waste, dressing in order to create an artificial impression, overindulgence in stimulants or in the brainwashing of perpetual TV, forming

[4]See Aulén, *Christus Victor*, pp. 33-34.

vulgar opinions as dictated by media, associating only with those people who constitute a social advantage to us — all this, and so much more, is worldly behavior. Can this be the work of the devil?. No screaming blasphemy and profanation, no dark and unspeakable deeds, but this? It is so normal .... Worse than that, it is endemic to us, bone of our bone and flesh of our flesh. Will we allow the addict or fiend to speak of the devil in his life? Why not the snob, the bore, the bigot, the cheat, the gossip? What about you and me? The evil which we fight, if we fight it at all, is not just the violent temptation that rushes at us. Screwtape and Wormwood attack us from within. Living with them as we do, we barely notice them. Unopposed, they have their way. The weakness and vice which are of our very nature, that constitute the person we know best — these are our worldly selves, these are souls to be redeemed. Bought back — from whom? From ourselves, from the shadow of death. "He has delivered us from the dominion of darkness and transferred us to the kingdom of his beloved Son, in whom we have redemption, the forgiveness of sins" (Col 1:13-14).

If we are to understand the death and resurrection of Jesus, we will best understand it as a struggle, not with an outside power, but with the human situation itself. That struggle takes place within the sphere of human experience and can be described in its terms. What Jesus did, in a word, was to pass through the whole spectrum of human suffering, including death. He had to draw all this suffering within himself and, again within himself, overcome that suffering. He had, finally, to give us the opportunity of so being identified with him that his victory might also be ours.

I had long been looking for an image to express this conception. I was attracted to an ancient Christian theme, evoked by the liturgical adaptation at Christmas of a passage from Wisdom: "While gentle silence enveloped all things, and night in its swift course was now half gone, thy all-powerful word leaped from heaven..." (Wis 18:14-15).[5] The picture here is of the *Logos* slipping unperceived from its privileged place in the heavens, down through all the aeons, the lesser stages, until it reached earth, still as it were in disguise and now in the form of man. Down further it went, to the bottom of things, but then it rose, this time in splendor, triumphantly, back through all those aeons to the place from where it had come. In this context, the psalm verse, "Who is this King of Glory? The Lord of hosts, he is the king of glory" (Ps 24:10), is seen as the bewildered dialogue of the princes of the air who have lost their hold on man because they did not recognize the Lord while he was a humble man. In his itinerary, Jesus has claimed all that he visited, even the depths of hell. In his flesh, he has made those depths his, and in rising he has raised up all flesh.

> In saying, "He ascended," what does it mean but that he had also descended into the lower parts of the earth? He who descended is he who also ascended far above all the heavens, that he might fill all things (Eph 4:9-10).

So far so good: the perspective of myth. The New Testament also expresses the same idea with psychological insight. Jesus can raise us up because he has made all our suffering his.

[5]For what follows, see Jean Daniélou, *The Bible and the Liturgy* (Notre Dame, 1956), pp. 304-307.

"He can deal gently with the ignorant and wayward, since he himself is beset with weakness. . . . Although he was a Son, he learned obedience through what he suffered, and being made perfect he became the source of salvation to all who obey him" (Hb 5:2, 8). This sharing of our condition went all the way to despair, to the calling out at Gethsemane to an absent God who had forsaken him (Mt 26:39; 27:46).

Still, with students in mind, I was looking for a more contemporary image to express this good news. I found one recently, where I least expected it. The documentary film *Scared Straight* shows a group of juvenile delinquents on a visit to a prison, listening to talks from convicts, most of them serving life sentences. While I was fascinated by the effect on the adolescents of the prisoners' speeches, I was even more interested in the prisoners themselves. For an hour these men harangued, menaced, and terrified their young listeners. In their own vile language, they portrayed prison life as the hell it is — the cruelty, the injustice, the sexual and psychological abuse. The young people heard of the treatment of young prisoners by the veterans, a tale of intimidation, slavery, and sometimes execution.

Having never visited a prison or talked with a convict, I may have received a greater shock than the teenagers who were there. More than those frightened boys and girls, I felt totally alienated from these men of brutal face, strident voice, and stinging language. I saw them as men from another world.

At the end of the program, however, the same convicts talked privately with the interviewer. The tough masks fell as the men explained their sense of mission in saving young people from a life of crime and imprisonment. There was one prisoner whose lecture to the juveniles had been particularly horrifying. He now explained that, as a believing Christian, his talking to young people was his form of missionary work. Suddenly my feelings of alienation took a very different turn. Not only were these men my brothers as humans and my brothers in Christ, but they were also performing a priestly work of redemption which I, a priest, would never be capable of doing.

"So these men seem strange to you?" I thought. Then I thought, "How do we all look to God?" I see those men, and I wonder what Christian charity might prompt me to do for their good. Giving a contribution, or anything that didn't involve going into the prison? Conceivably. Becoming a prison chaplain? I've never done anything like that, but if I were called to it, perhaps I could. What about actually becoming a prisoner and ministering from within, on the model of the worker priests? *Nobody* would do that. Nobody? Well, you can always find a saint for everything. I remember, as a child, seeing *Monsieur Vincent* and the moment when Vincent dePaul jumps into the stinking ranks of galley slaves to replace a man being beaten, but even there one knew he didn't remain a galley slave. There were saints in the wars of this century, such as Maximilian Kolbe, who offered themselves in place of those about to die. Still, we don't have many heroes who volunteered for confinement. Now imagine such a person who enters prison, not as a substitute for someone else, but to redeem and save all the prisoners from within?

If prisoners, my own fellow men, seem so alien and terrible to me, how might the world of sinful men look to God? My sensibilities are offended by what I see and hear of prison, but what happens in a prison that does not happen elsewhere?

Where is there not cruelty, bestiality, extortion, quarreling, corruption? These men are criminals, virtually all of them from that part of society from which criminals are likely to come. Sinners come from all social classes, and it is not for us to suppose that the worst criminals are also the worst sinners. As in the case of the publican and pharisee, the heart of a given convict may be more pleasing to God than the impenitent heart of a given judge.

What we see in the congregated evil of a prison is, then, but a faint analogy to what we may imagine God to have experienced when he entered into the confinement of the flesh. "Though he was in the form of God, he did not count equality with God a thing to be grasped, but emptied himself, taking the form of a slave, being born in the likeness of men . . ." (Phil 2:6-7). The straitened circumstances of Jesus' life — the stable, the hiddenness, the mission to just a few fishing villages — are themselves only a reminder of the anguish of exchanging divinity for the sphere of sinfulness. "He who knew no sin became sin for our sake" (2 Cor 5:21).

To make a parable of it, imagine the world Jesus enters as a great circular prison, designed in concentric circles. From above, it looks like a riflery target or archery butt. Each circle represents a level of the human condition. Jesus must enter at the outside, at the mere fact of being born, and he must pass through, circle by circle, until he reaches the center. In Dante's hell the roads wind, corkscrew fashion, but in this prison the only way from circle to circle is through a door which unlocks only from the outside. You can go in, but you can't come out. Every crime and every sin has its place, with every kind of suffering. Jesus keeps going in, experiencing it all. Finally he reaches the center, where execution takes place. Perhaps he is executed by the authorities, perhaps by the prisoners themselves. He goes through it all, and dies.

Now imagine the prison, not as the totality of the world's ills, but as the whole experience of one person. The outermost ring is the edge of consciousness, where the world begins to form a part of our world. It is our ambition to expand that outer ring, to extend ourselves out into the world. Think of the constriction that God now undergoes, limiting himself to one human consciousness in the person of Jesus. As man, his life history was typically human: first expansion, but then contraction. To be fulfilled is to expand, but to suffer is to experience the shrinking of the circles.[6] A headache prevents us from reading, sadness from conversation, monotony from creation. Instead of expanding, we withdraw. We want consciousness of our world; intead we get consciousness of ourselves, of our pain or of our boredom. Intense suffering is a more terrible pressing of the consciousness in on itself, where nothing is known but the pain. The final moment comes when consciousness withdraws to its center and collapses inwardly. There is no further experience of the world around. The light goes out. It is death. The center is the person, the focal point of our life and consciousness. We are organized around this center, the inner source of our identity. It is from here that we expand, and to this that we return. As Jesus hung on the cross, he returned to his center. His suffering caved in at this core, but the light could not go out because that center, the person of Jesus, was the divine person. Jesus' humanity

---

[6]To understand this better, see above, p. 27: "To be myself is to be conscious, and to be conscious is to focus on anything other than myself."

was organized around God as its still center, but that could only become apparent in the ultimate event of the total return to the center, death. *Consummatum est.* It is finished. He gave up the spirit and brought human experience to its end.

Because of the divine center, Jesus' death could only be a beginning, a rising, a new assertion of what humanity now is. What is essential here is that it really did happen. If this man did not in fact leave his tomb, then the theology of Resurrection is a foolish deception. It either happened or it didn't. If it happened, as I believe it did, then there is this: instead of collapse at the center, there is re-emergence. Jesus goes back through all those circles, opening all the doors from within. As each door flies open, and stays open, the guards and prisoners remember the downcast man who passed through before, going the way from which no-one ever returns. "Who is this King of glory?" Jesus can free all the prisoners because he has gone himself to unlock their doors. If they wish to follow him out, they can live in a reality where they are no longer confined by their sins, and where their center is not the point of death, but rather the flame of life.

As in Plato's cave, it is important that the vehicle of the prison should bear two kinds of meaning.[7] After I see the prison as a world, I see it as myself. The parable begins as a myth but ends as a mirror, a method of analysis. My personality, like my heart, expands and retracts. I go out to the world, and I draw it in to myself. Always there remains that center, not to be touched until the final moment of death; it is the center of my consciousness. Is there anything in my experience which I can allow to enter me, and to come all the way

[7]Plato, *Republic*, VII.514-521.

back to my center? I am afraid to answer the question. I sense that the center is myself, and that to give up this privileged "I," to allow another being to occupy that final space, would constitute a kind of death, an abandonment of my individuality. On the other hand, I also sense that "I" am not self-sufficient, that my center, although the source of my consciousness, is not the source of my existence. "I" am a center of nothingness, a point of collapse and death. My real center is the source of my being, which is not "I" but God. What does God ask? That I allow him to be at my center of consciousness, to occupy my ego, he who is my real center. I can do this by believing in Jesus as Lord. In his death, Jesus goes to the center. He relinquishes the center which is his human self, his "I," and then rises. He is still himself, he has lost nothing, but his true center is now the being of God. Nothing has been lost, and all has been gained. The displacement of the self has been accomplished in Jesus. By putting our faith in him, we allow Jesus to come back to our center, "to live by faith in our hearts" (Eph 3:17). As a result, we die to our false ego and gain our true self. Belief in the death and Resurrection of Jesus, which really happened and now really happens to us, is *the* saving event. "Amen, Amen I say to you, unless a grain of wheat falls into the earth and dies, it remains alone; but if it dies, it bears much fruit" (Jn 12:24).

I can understand this text well enough in its application to Jesus, but now I must understand it as applying to me. Does it mean that I accept Jesus by imitating his death? That I am the grain of wheat? The metaphor of grain and earth reminds me of the parable of the sower who went out to sow. In that parable, by Jesus' interpretation, the seed is the Word of God and we, the listeners, are the earth which receives that Word

(Mk 4:13-20). I sense the same point here. Jesus must die in us and, rising, bear fruit in us. It is not enough that Jesus did die and rise, although the reality of those events is indispensable. Now I must accept these events into myself through faith. I am the prison, I am the earth. "Behold, I stand at the door and knock; if anyone hears my voice and opens the door, I will come in to him and eat with him, and he with me" (Rev 3:20).

Of course this acceptance is also a death for us, the displacement of the false center of "I" by the new, rising-in-me center which is the being of God. Our life in sin, as in Plato's cave, is one based on unreality, the illusory self. It is to this illusion, myself as source of being, that I unreasonably cling. To believe and to accept is to let go.

Thorton Wilder's *Bridge of San Luis Rey* presents what amounts to a masque of this saving event, the rope bridge over the chasm which unpredictably snaps, hurling five travelers into the chasm beneath. What destiny had brought them all to the bridge at just that moment? It was, we discover, that all five had just learned, after a bitter struggle, the lesson of relinquishment, that they should no longer cling to possession of a person or *idée fixe*. Each one, having untied the heart's knot and at last breathed the fresh air of evening peace, is now prepared to break all the ties.

Sometimes the accident comes first. I know a young man, Peter, who fell out a window last winter. It was an absurd accident, resulting in a headlong fall to the pavement thirty feet below. Head injuries and a snapped spinal cord: paralysis for life from the waist down.

Up to that moment, Peter's life had been a whirlwind of activity. He had most of the things he wanted — money, good looks, all kinds of ability — and unlimited supplies of energy and ambition to acquire what he didn't yet have. His life was worldly and fast-moving, and he enjoyed it with intensity. Serious about work, he was aiming at success in a very large family business. His values were totally secular. He did not believe in God, and at school he sometimes taunted a pious roommate. He was capable of zany humor and fierce rage, was headstrong, colorful, and very confident. After a year, he moved to a different school.

Then he fell. It took Peter several weeks to regain consciousness, and after that he had to be told about his legs. I had the worst fears over what I thought his reaction to the truth would be. To my amazement, when I went to visit him, I found a new Peter. He was peaceful, gentle, full of happiness and determination to finish his education and do everything he could within his limitations. He told me that he now believed in God. I then discovered that the hospital chaplain had come to see him as soon as he had recovered his consciousness, and asked Peter if he could pray with him. Peter didn't mind, but as he lay there he thought the whole thing was foolish. Still, the priest prayed, and then he came back the next day and prayed again. After a day or two, it occurred to Peter that perhaps prayer wasn't so foolish after all. He made friends with the chaplain, and began to discover belief in God for the first time in his life. It made all the difference. He smiled as he told me all this, and said, "I'll bet my old roommate would be surprised to see me now."

In the months that followed, I would visit him at the Spinal Cord Institute in Boston. Many of the paraplegics there are as young as Peter, victims of automobile or ski accidents. One gets the sense of life abruptly halted — vacant faces smoking cigarettes, speaking in hushed tones, perhaps still wondering,

"Why me?" Peter had lost none of his old dynamism, and was now using it in different ways, entering wheelchair races, buying presents to cheer up fellow patients, energetically planning for the future. He completed his therapy in record time, and moved to a house in Boston from where he resumed his education. Why Peter? How has God acted toward him? Has he really thrown him down, to pick him up again and remake him? Can I believe that Peter is one of God's chosen ones?

I say and believe that God is at work in Peter, although I do not know why he fell. I don't know why anyone falls, or why there are epidemics, famine, or war. What I see in Peter is falling, descent to the lowest point, and a return to a new life. When I pray, "Lead us not into temptation," I am asking God not to put me to the test, not to lead me to the point where, in despair, I would no longer be able to trust him. I grope and hesitate, while others, like Peter, are chosen to reenact the Passion and Resurrection. "Let those who can take it, take it" (Mt 19:12).

I see in Peter, the convert, what I must be every day. "Repent, and believe the gospel." The forty days end with the Resurrection. Repentance ends with conversion, but this turning to God is something that must go on every day. I stand between my self-centeredness and the center of God, between nothingness and being, between shadows and light. "Lead us not into temptation, but deliver us from evil." Since Jesus has really died and risen, my not-being need not be the place of my death. I can relinquish the false self, and rise to new being. When I see it happening to Peter, and to young people here, I know it can happen, even daily, to me and to many others. I thank God for this time of grace.

6

Time to be going: Pentecost

And when they had come opposite Mysia, they attempted to go
into Bythynia, but the Spirit of Jesus did not allow them; so,
passing by Mysia, they went down to Troas. And a vision
appeared to Paul in the night: a man of Macedonia was standing
beseeching him and saying, "Come over to Macedonia and help
us." And when he had seen the vision, immediately we sought
to go on into Macedonia, concluding that God had called us to
preach the gospel to them (Ac 16:6-10).

The liturgical year is a drama of past and present. Its central
mysteries, birth and resurrection, are events that happened
once and for all in specific places and times. Now they are also
events in our lives, in our personal histories of grace, and so in
the liturgy we make *anamnesis*, we call to mind and make the
past present. What might have been lost is not lost; it is actual,
now.

At Pentecost, again, we commemorate an event, the giving
of the Holy Spirit to the apostles, but this event by its nature is
always in the present. Pentecost was the day that the Holy

Spirit first came to the Church, but it has been coming every day since then. As we gather to pray at Pentecost, we must be fully, keenly aware of the present possibility. *Veni, Sancte Spiritus*: Come, Holy Spirit, fill the hearts of your people. Just suppose our prayer was answered; what would happen?

What are we really praying for? We could hardly pray for more than, in fact, Jesus has promised us in his gift of the Spirit. When the Spirit comes, we are to do greater works even than Jesus. The Holy Spirit will teach us all things, the total teaching of Jesus. In the Spirit we have the mind of Christ. All that was Christ's is to be ours, through the Spirit. We know that this is reality, although we treat it as rhetoric. Why, asked St. Paul, if Jesus rose from the dead and gave us eternal life, would he not give us everything else besides? We share in his death and resurrection, we live God's life. Yes, we sense something happening within us, the life of the Spirit. The year of grace is this: to know, day by day, that the old self is dying, the rampant ego and its tyranny of demands, and that the new self, the whole person recreated by the spirit of God, is being born in its place.

Pentecost comes, most years, at about the time of our school graduation, the time that everyone leaves. Or call it commencement, a new beginning. I recall Jesus' last words to his followers, "Go, therefore."

Our seniors try to act as though they felt euphoria, doing their best to mask their real feelings of loss and doubt. They may not have realized until the last few weeks how deep their friendships were, and today they know that they may never see some of these friends again in this life. Their families are here, but they are not really going home. Summer will only be an interval. After that lies the unknown, a truly new beginning.

For us who remain, it is the same event each year, *anamnesis*, except that each time we are a year older. I would be unmoved by the event if I had never grown close to the students. Or, if I had grown too close, it would be, for me too, a terrible time of loss. I try to be neither indifferent nor upset. Teaching is a wonderful discipline, an *ascesis* which teaches the teacher to love only by giving, asking nothing in return, never grasping, holding, or clinging. ("You have let us down," says the angry teacher to the student in disgrace. What right had he to say that? Let the student be punished — it is his right — but not for having failed to live up to a teacher's self-interested and, therefore, distorted image of him.) Yes, you and I were close to each other for these few years. There were times of conflict and times of mutual aid, times of understanding and affection. Now, though, you are leaving, and for your sake and for mine, I am very glad. You will grow, and so will I. Good-bye and God bless you! "Later! We're so outta here!" And he goes: I'm not sure where to, and I doubt that he is sure either. I look forward to meeting his younger brother in the fall.

The year of grace becomes years of graces. I started to write this book in 1979, when I was forty. I wrote of Epiphany, the first cycle of desire, and I looked back at my childhood. I am now 44, and have come back to this book to write of Pentecost, the end of the second cycle. I think it had to be this way. Four years ago, the wheel had just begun to turn for the second time. I knew that then, because I could feel it, but I had no idea how fast or how far it would turn. The first cycle, that of desire and knowledge, is the cycle of youth, the time of reaching out, being called, and setting forth. The second cycle is the time of life and death. I suppose it can happen anytime, but mid-life is one of its privileged moments. Therefore, it is happening now.

What of the intervening time, the *entre deux guerres*? A man's twenties, says Levinson,[1] are the time of apprenticeship; the thirties are the period of emerging, of becoming someone of ability, of being recognized. In the forties, of course, all that went before is called into question.

I came to Portsmouth at the age of 21 and, at 25, had the good fortune to be sent to the Benedictine College in Rome for four years of study. There were such riches — the great city, the good theological training, the friendship of monks, young and old, from many parts of the world. Now, though, I see how many of those opportunities I ignored, unable for so long to think of anything but one abiding thought: "What will I become?" It seems a silly question, for someone who has made monastic vows — we call it monastic profession. For all that I take my vows seriously, I have never been able to think of myself as a professional monk. "Career," then, was my key word. No-one in those Roman days, absolutely no-one was telling me I needed a career. Nothing could have been further from the American ethos of success than a Roman monastery, and yet there it was, a persistent *daimon*, a nagging voice: "What are you in the eyes of the world? What will you become?"

[1]Daniel Levinson, *The Seasons of a Man's Life* (N.Y.: Ballantine, 1979).

I thought of myself as a scholar and developed an area of interest at which I worked for two or three years with unbounded zeal. It was, indeed, a happy time. Thursday mornings at the Vatican Library were the high point of my week. I read and read, endlessly collecting minutiae, and even doing some original work for publication. I wrote to famous scholars and, in the summer, travelled to see them. I even started to make arrangements for going on, after Rome, to do a doctorate at Oxford. My community, however, had other ideas. They told me to come home and teach, and so I did as I was told without, as I remember, a trace of regret.

The abbot, says St. Benedict, is believed to hold the place of Christ in the monastery. Obedience, therefore, is an act of receiving the Holy Spirit. So often we do not know what we want, what is best for us. Going for a doctorate would have been, I now see, a disaster. Professional scholarship was not my vocation. I also see, with painful clarity, what I could have seen then if I had looked honestly: that I was less interested in my scholarly subject than in being recognized as an expert in that subject. For me, the thing itself was always subordinate to my role in dealing with it, and that is why I could never be a true scholar. The self-centered ego is self defeating. The terms of its demands insure that those demands will never be satisfied. It took years for me to stop playing this tragi-comic role; some who know me well might say that I am still playing it.

As I turned thirty, then, I returned home to teach, and was quickly given the name "zealot" by students who could not believe that anyone could be as enthusiastic as I about the French language. I have never minded the name, and I think now that I understand it. It seems odd, at first, that someone so dogged by self-consciousness in one pursuit should earn a reputation for reckless abandon in another, but it makes sense to me. Teaching, after such a crabbed preoccupation with self, was a wonderful therapy, a clean stream of pure energy to dispel the selfish murk. In any case, I have taught zealously for fifteen years.

The ego, of course, is not so easily fooled. It wants only the gratification of a role played successfully, applauded by an appreciative audience. Never mind how — the role can just as well be a teacher's as a scholar's. One can even play coach, administrator, housemaster, and advisor, although playing them all at once, as I was to find out, is unwise. Wheels spin, energy is expended. There is a growing sense of good intentions, and even good results, and with this growth, always, the ego continues to grow. So good are the intentions that an inner censor makes sure that the only feedback to be permitted will be positive, such as to reinforce the good feelings. Negative vibrations are drowned out in the internal whir. Worst of all, the well-meaning and busy egotist is barred from any accurate understanding of other people. I welcomed everyone, and wanted to know and help as many students as I could, but always on my terms. The ego surrounds itself with people, shaping and molding them, recreating them in its own image. The seventies, my thirties, were good years, useful and constructive ones, and yet, as I look back at them, I am appalled at my ignorance. I wonder if it will be the same, ten years from now? If I will again wonder how I could have been so blind? In a way, I hope so.

The year of grace, then, is the year you turn forty — or just let it be the year you experience breakup and change. The classic crisis of the male at forty is his disillusionment with activity and achievement, a questioning of its meaning and purpose, even panic at the impending loss of youth and vitality. Years ago, in Rome, Fr. Anselm Günthör had taught us the term *Torschlusspanik*, the panic at the closing of the door. Like Faust, many try to recreate their youth, and fail, or abandon their life styles and start new ones. A change is indeed necessary, but it must first be an inward one. Without it, no change of scenery, task, or companions will do the slightest good.

I think Jesus was talking directly to American males of middle age when he said, "What does it profit a man if he gain the whole world and suffer the loss of his soul?" I agree with Carl Jung, who takes "soul" here to mean the unconscious, inner life, our abiding point of contact with the transcendent. Through those twenty years when we pursued achievement, we repressed the unconscious, drowned it in our frenzy of over-conscious activity. The disillusioned man who, at middle age, has attained all his goals except happiness, has gained the world and lost his soul. And so he begins the search for identity, real being. It is often a painful process in which bonds are broken and commitments dishonored. Married men are divorced and priests get married. Each year, as the pressures to achieve in America increase, it is logical to expect that mid-life crisis will become a greater and greater agony, made greater still by the concomitant decline in sexual self-discipline.

It is no easy thing to write about one's own mid-life, since the essence of that experience is to play the fool. This time for me is a tribunal in which my past is reviewed, and I am told, "Your desire for dignity, your *amour-propre*, has made you inhuman. Will you continue to wrap your pride around you like a cloak? If so, you are condemned to a sad and lonely old age. No? You wish to live again? Then you must remove your cloak and dance, naked, before all those whose respect you have labored to command." One is glad to accept the sentence. David danced naked before the Ark, and was despised by his wife. Only, in our day, it is more difficult. We have almost forgotten the Feast of Fools and so, when the sacred dance is imposed, it seems a harsh sentence.

Yet let it begin. When I was about forty, I went to my first charismatic prayer meeting. That seems nothing much, now, but at the time it was very new and strange to me. Like most of my confreres at Portsmouth, I tend to be a traditionalist at public liturgies. *Gravitas* is a distinguishing feature of our Roman rite, and we should strive to keep it. I prefer rubrics to spontaneous whims, plainsong to pop. Despite all this, at my first prayer meeting, I rejoiced to find myself praying spontaneously, praying out loud. For me, it was a simple but genuine breakthrough. Something came through the crust; emotions were released and began to flow. In my daily life, and with the students, they continued to flow in this new found spiritual enthusiasm. Sometimes they overflowed. That's what it is to play the fool, but so be it. I think of Bergman's classic film, *The Seventh Seal*, which ends with the *Totentanz*, the dance of death in which all, rich or poor, high or low, must skip and prance, up and up the hillside to the great destiny which awaits them. This is the dance of mid-life crisis. *Krisis*, after all, means judgment, and it is the judgment of Jesus that we should join the dance. "Now is the judgment of the world" (*krisis tou kosmou* — you could say "crisis of the cosmos"), "now the ruler of this world is cast out, and I, if I be lifted up, will draw all people to myself."

The Charismatic movement, then, was a first step. I went to prayer meetings for about a year. I knew all the time that it would neither be possible nor desirable to merge this religious style with the more sober rhythms of my monastic life. Then too, there was the nagging thought that the Holy Spirit should never be the possession of a group. I met a young woman, a convert, who said she had received both baptisms at the same time, the second being Baptism in the Holy Spirit. I couldn't understand that — do we not, precisely, receive the Holy Spirit in Baptism and Confirmation? Should we tell baptized Christians that they must receive the Spirit? They have the Spirit: our job, as apostles, is to help them discover it within themselves. With a movement of spirituality in the Church replacing the older evangelical movements, this seems to be a shared opinion. Perhaps the Charismatic movement in the Church has had its heyday. Perhaps I am just constitutionally chary of movements. I, in any case, received a great gift at those meetings. I was opened to the Holy Spirit.

Then, in the same year, I made my first pilgrimage to Lourdes. It was not my first trip there. Over ten years before, during my student years in Europe, I had spent a night at a nearby Benedictine monastery. I was expecting to have two hours in Lourdes, a place that I then had little inclination to see. I asked the guestmaster to recommend the best way to visit the shrine. He said, "Go straight to the Grotto. Do not look to the left or to the right until you get there, and when you do, just sit in silence until it is time to leave. While you are there, you will feel the spirit of the place, which is miraculous." It was early June, and there were few people there. I followed my directions, and it was just as he said. I felt a moving stillness within me which I never forgot.

Now, in 1979, I was invited by a kind alumnus of our school to join him and some current students as part of a large pilgrimage which goes every summer to Lourdes from England under the auspices of Ampleforth Abbey. I went, not knowing that it was to be the first of five times.

We don't have pilgrimages in the United States and, generally, we don't know what they are. It is not our way to make holy voyages. I wonder if this isn't a symptom of that disease whereby we have gained the world and lost our souls. Of course it is true that, at the time of writing, Our Lady has not yet appeared in the United States. Imagine her, standing on Plymouth Rock and talking to a pilgrim father!

The uninitiated American must, then, imagine a small town jam-packed with happy pilgrims, the well pushing the sick about in *voitures*. Ampleforth, with its fifty sick and one hundred helpers, is one of the smaller groups. My own duties were partly priestly and partly those of a helper, caring for the sick in the hospital and helping to carry them to the activities of each day during our week together. Like most people who come on a pilgrimage for the first time, I had no first-hand experience of serious illness, and was frankly apprehensive at the thought of what I might have to see or do.

When the sick arrived at the hospital on that first night, though, I quickly forgot my fear and was absorbed in what had to be done. By the time we had gotten them all to bed I found myself, by a strange circumstance, volunteered for the night shift, and so I stayed until six the next morning. Three things happened to me that night. First one of the ladies, a poor person from London, had lost her luggage and was almost hysterical. When, after several difficult hours, we had reunited her with her suitcase and put her to bed, I helped to calm her by praying with her. Then around midnight, a male patient, a heavy man with both legs amputated, had to be attended to. All the grubby things I had feared were now staring me in the face. The nurse helped me with instructions, and the patient encouraged me with a running stream of kindness and jokes. When we were finished I felt wonderful. (It was the patient's first pilgrimage, too, and his last. Two nights later, at about the same time, he had a seizure and died.) Finally, in the small hours, other helpers and I sat over coffee and talked, talked in an intimate way as though we had been lifelong friends. That, in one night, was all of Lourdes: love in prayer, love in caring for the sick, and love in friendship. The young helpers, strong enough to burn the candle at both ends, spend their days with the sick, their evenings with each other and, well after midnight, they end with a quiet and often long visit to the Grotto.

The truly amazing thing about Lourdes is the way that these three elements — prayer, charity, and friendship; religion, works, and celebration —all fuse into one experience. Our forebears, those puritan pilgrims, could not reconcile anything worthwhile with simple enjoyment, certainly not religion. But so it is at Lourdes and, I imagine, in heaven too. That is why we go there, to learn the unity of things.

Again and again, at Lourdes, I have seen them come as I came: narrow and cramped, timidly arriving in fear of self, fear of sickness, fear of others, fear of God. Then the miracles begin to occur, curing that deep inner disease of the sick self, the lost soul. They all come, the unbelieving and the superstitious, the worriers and the despairing, the manipulators and the victimized, the angry and the lost. They come and they experience, all day and all night, the energy of love. They meet the saints, those men and women who live in perpetual pain and the companionship of death. They reverently wash the naked bodies of these holy ones, they strip themselves before putting on a soggy towel to go into the freezing water of the baths, they disclose their hearts in a hoped-for but unexpected conversation, perhaps in the small hours of the morning. Then they discover, almost without caring, that they too are dancing nakedly. Perfect love casts out fear.

In the early seventies I began to offer a Senior course in philosophy, and I have been giving it ever since. It starts with the great Greco-Roman tradition; we read Plato, Augustine, Aquinas. We study the Enlightenment challenge to that tradition and some of the reactions to the challenge. Hume and Kant are discussed, Pascal and Kierkegaard read. Finally, in the spring, our job is to see if the old tradition can be expressed in terms that have any meaning for us in the twentieth century. Here, the books most helpful to us have been Mounier's *Personalism*,[2] E. F. Schumacher's *Guide for the Perplexed*,[3] and Jung's *Memories, Dreams, Reflections*. Metaphysics is still alive, but what was once a world view must now, I think, be translated as a view of personality. What I have discovered, in the last few years, is that the spring term of this course tends to change from philosophy to spirituality. At first this surprised me, and it surprised me even more to see that this development made sense to the students. Jung's own quarrel with conventional Christianity (his father had been a minister) centered on the question of spiritual experience. His inner life

[2]Emmanuel Mounier, *Personalism* (Notre Dame, 1970).

[3]E. F. Schumacher, *Guide for the Perplexed* (N.Y.: Harper and Row, 1978).

— dreams, fantasies, thoughts — was rich with symbols and themes of the Holy. By contrast, the doctrines and rites of the official Church seemed merely formal, unable to engage the feelings even of those who performed them. Could it be that our own students, growing up in a secular world and often uncomfortable with our Christian ethos of sacraments and doctrine, live nevertheless in a grace-filled inner world, a world which, perhaps, they have never seen or experienced?

Once I became aware of this, the evidence started to gather. Students sometimes speak up at informal retreats, revealing spiritual lives of great depth. From time to time, in class, we do visual exercises such as drawing mandalas or exercises in active imagination. When a student has done a mandala — filled in a circle with random designs — he and I stare at it together, asking questions and making suggestions, helping each other to discover meaning. It takes time, but usually meanings come, and they are often impressive. A student who had earlier been in the hospital found in his drawing a fear of death and separation from his family, and was able to accept and even bless a reality which before had been dogging his footsteps. We call active imagination "fantasy journeys." Students narrate their wanderings — flying, swimming, falling through an inner landscape. They enjoy it, and it is certainly more interesting than the standard fantasy literature that clutters many of their bookshelves. Some of them just occasionally come to places of peace, awareness, and happiness which, I hope, they will not soon forget.

A few of them have learned to meditate, although most of those who try it, at that age, still find it difficult. Keeping the body quiet in sitting and the mind quiet in centering is a challenge for those whose bodies and minds are kept all day long in intense and fatiguing activity. We occasionally do some simple yoga, relaxation and breathing exercises, and sometimes a few moments of spiritual centering are won.

It is difficult to do these things without acquiring the label of faddist. I personally do not teach Eastern thought for the simple reason that I do not understand it. That old Greco-Christian tradition is the one in which I live and move and have my being, and it is to its mysteries that I keep returning in admiration: the mystery of being as act (the constant creation of all being by God); the mystery of spiritual consciousness as soul, as the act of personal being which will survive death; and the crowning theological mystery of Spirit, a supernatural gift which grows out of natural consciousness and divinizes us, makes us godlike, even in this life. Yoga, meditation, and inner seeing are simply ways of experiencing our spiritual nature, our act of being. We are often told that we use only about 10% of our mental powers, but we are not told much that is positive about the remaining 90%. Is it part of our future? I had a student recently who thinks that ESP is the next step in human evolution. Or should we think of man as a little lower than the angels, enjoying one tenth of their powers but looking forward to fullness in the life to come? I am open to any suggestions, but this much I know: we have a spiritual life, and to become aware of it is to realize greater potential. I never met anyone who was not helped and gladdened by this realization. *Gratia supponit naturam.* There is a natural mysticism and a supernatural, the life of the soul and the life of the Spirit, meditation and prayer. We begin with our experience and we go on to "what eye has not seen nor ear heard, nor the heart of man conceived, what God has prepared for those who love him" (cf. 1 Cor 2:9).

Jung's own mid-life crisis coincided with his separation from Freud. Estranged from the master, to whom could he turn? He turned inward, to his own unconscious, deliberately and courageously journeying to greater depths than most of us have the capacity or desire to go. Spiritual guides came to him from within, as Virgil came to Dante, and led him on perilous paths to saving knowledge. My own journey, although vastly less profound or interesting than Jung's, has recently seemed to be leading me inward, where I had to walk alone, and where the knowledge of dreams, fantasies, and impulses became the material of self-revelation. I used to think such ventures introverted and morbid, at a time when I most suffered from the lack of self-knowledge. True encounter with the unconscious is in fact a path of deliverance from preoccupation with self, from that egotism and self-consciousness which plagued me through all those years of consuming and uncomprehending energy. Inner salvation is this: to be freed from the frenetic ritual of role-playing, the endless chase when we, pursued by our shadow, constantly contradict our best impulses in the name of the unsatisfied ego. To use Jung's terminology, the saving path is that of individuation, the passage from Ego to Self, from the demanding center which sets itself against all others, to the full Self, an integrated union of conscious and unconscious, of the independent reason and the Spirit within us, which embraces otherness and is one with it.

Pentecost coincides with graduation, the time of leaving and beginning. Patrick, a former student now at a large midwestern university, dropped in to visit one evening not long ago. When I saw him, I immediately thought of him as a Senior, hitting a single in a baseball game. He gave a visceral yell as he hit the ball, an "aagh!" like Jimmy Connors' service groan. It was just a short line drive over the shortstop's head, but Patrick gave it everything he had. He never studied very hard while he was here, but is now going full steam ahead in a very ambitious program of electrical engineering. We both remembered, as though it were yesterday, a long debate we had in philosophy class. He used to say that, even if there were no God, we would still pursue virtue just as though there were one; he agreed with Voltaire's "if there were no God we would have to invent one." I said that with atheism comes the loss of any real ground for morality; I agreed with Ivan Karamazov's "if God does not exist, anything is permitted." Now as we talked, though, I realized that I had completely misunderstood Patrick's point (or had it changed over these two years?). Now, at any rate, he was not saying that belief in God is not necessary for virtue. He only meant that, even if we do not refer to God or believe in him philosophically, he is still within us, and there he can be sought and found.

We talked on about his fascination for Einstein and the mysteries of relativity, and compared these insights about reality to those of the mystics. He still continues, he said, the little bit of meditation which he started here, usually when he needs to compose himself before exams. We spent a pleasant two hours together, the first one talking and the second doing relaxation exercises and sitting together in silence. When Patrick left, we both knew during which hour there had been the greatest communication.

Patrick leaves, and as he does I see some of my most cherished ideas crumbling to dust. What do I know about people? I am a "two cultures" man, forever setting up technology and spirituality in opposition to each other. Yet here is this young man who, had I really listened to him two years ago, might have taught me some things about the God within. How did he find his way to my door this evening? Now he is back on a road which leads, he hopes, either to Boston's route 128 or to California's Silicon Valley, the empires of hi-tech. Such success will be, for him, a sign of inner development, expansion of the Spirit, the power of God.

My edifice of thought is down all around me now. I have long thought — and talked — about the relationship of school and monastery, and the ideas have always come in contrasting pairs: the gospel and the world, the sacred and the secular, Jerusalem and Athens. I know how to preach and can, on demand, be eloquent. I can compare the strictures of college admissions with the strait gate and the needle's eye. We develop these dualisms, of course, only to confound ourselves, for if there are these contradictions, it is we, the monks, who embody them.

What would happen if, when we have meetings and set policies, all were to sit in silence for a few minutes as Patrick and I did? I think we would discover that our ideas, our theories, are more apparent than real. Of course there is a "sacred" and a "secular," but our task is the salvation of one by the other, not their eternal opposition. Now is the judgment of the world, true, and now the Prince of this world is cast out, true again. But this is truest of all: I, if I be lifted up, will draw all people to myself. And how will we lift him up? How will we draw others to Him? Through his gift of the Spirit.

My monastic vocation is a contemplative one. This inner work of prayer, the lifting up of the Lord within me, is at the very heart of my calling. What right have I to theorize that this "sacred" element in my life stands opposed to the "secularity" of the school and its scholars? My call is, precisely, through contemplation to redeem the time, because the days are evil. My witness to that world is through my contemplative life, and it is through that life more than any other that I can touch the world with the power of God. As monks we still have, and must keep, what we have always had: our liturgy, our observance, our doctrine. We lead students in worship, we try to set an example of Christian living, we teach Christian doctrine. Yet that is not enough. I suspect, in fact, that these elements are not now the ones to which the students can respond most readily. There is something else: God within us, the presence of the Holy Spirit in our hearts and in the hearts of all who believe. *Cor ad cor loquitur.* That was Cardinal Newman's motto, and it might well be ours. A monastic school in a secular world: what is that but a challenge to monks to go to their deepest origin, to draw their most powerful tools from the workshop of the monastery? Whether we like it or not, we find that we are missionary monks whose success or failure depends on the power of the Spirit, the authenticity of our contemplation. *Cor ad cor.* We, in monastery and school, are called to be a community of hearts, open to each other, listening and speaking, in word, action, and silence, of the ways God is acting in us.

Pentecost is the time of graduation, of commencement. People leave each year, and we begin again. We are on a journey, we make fresh starts. This is the condition of our lives, of those pilgrimages whose goal is the temple where we will be filled with the fullness of the Spirit. This is everyone's goal. "And they were *all* filled with the power of the Holy

Spirit." Sanctity is simply the Christian way of life. Paul writes
to the saints at Corinth, even to scold them for their misbehav-
ior. The Spirit is poured into our hearts through faith. This is
no gnostic teaching, no esoteric doctrine for a privileged few.
To think so is to have experienced nothing of the Spirit. The
further I journey inward and the closer I come to the life of the
Spirit within me, the closer I come to all those around me, to
all those whom I am called to touch. They, all of them, are also
in the Spirit. *Cor ad cor loquitur.* Our last common language is
the language of the Spirit in the heart, and our last educational
task is to learn that language together.

> The Spirit of the Lord God is upon me,
>   because the Lord has anointed me
> to bring good tidings to the afflicted;
>   he has sent me to bind the brokenhearted,
> to proclaim liberty to the captives,
>   and the opening of the prison to those who are bound;
> to proclaim the year of the Lord's favor.

At length, then, I have learned what the year of grace
brings. It is the year of release, the undoing of chains. First the
chains of ego, which keep us from our Selves. Then the chains
of ignorance, which keep us from God in our Selves. Finally,
the chains of fear, which keep us from others in God. How
good God is, and how gently he leads us through time!

Epilogue

Kairos

"My heart speaks for you and says, 'Seek my face.'
Your face, Lord, will I seek" (Ps 27:10).

Time is a unit of being, a mode of discovery. I reached out, I was touched, I encountered a presence. I was young. I turned, I came to the center of death and life, I was inwardly reborn. I grew older. It does not matter when. These are times, ways of meeting God, seasons of the Church's year, motions of the heart.

I think that these three *kairoi* are the three ways that God lets us know him. First there is the time of God the Father, the time when God is over-arching but distant. We were children, and he was above us. We grew older, and found that he is "under the world's splendor and wonder." We reach out in desire to unknown happiness, or withdraw in fear from unknown severity. This is the God of law, of the objective order which must be as it is and which I can do nothing to change, the one who is right when I am wrong. It is the quiet power of love, always waiting for me to return to it.

Then there is the *kairos* of God the Son, a person like me. I can see him, standing next to me. He talks to me, he is right there. He touches me. His time is the time of specific

129

moments, the particular days that are all important to me. I can listen to his words, and they change my life. In a way, this God is harder to believe in than the first because he suffers, but in a way easier because he is always there. He is a friend that I can love, a master that I can follow. His is the *kairos* of birth, of death, and again of birth. He touches me.

In the history of salvation, the first *kairos*, that of Israel, was the time of the Father. It was long, and it led to the *kairos* of Jesus, the Son. This was the absolute, the particular moment when time and eternity met. Now the third *kairos* is that of the Holy Spirit, the God within me. Like the first God, I cannot see him, but like the second, he is very close. More invisible even than the first, and even closer than the second. He is not the God of special moments because he is always present. He fills me with being, with light, with power. I do not understand him because I do not understand myself, but to know myself is to know him. He speaks best in silence. He is love, and knits me to others. He is strong and unforeseen, like the wind that he is: so the future is always becoming the present, and each leave-taking is a new beginning.

So I must speak, but these are not three Gods. There is but one God in three persons, infinite in three times, perfectly still in three endlessly interpenetrating motions, "a music that has neither beginning nor end."[1]

This time, God's time, is the best time.

---

[1]"Leonard Bernstein, perhaps the last person to speak with Nadia Boulanger..asked if she heard music in her head, and if so, what music. ...she answered from afar: 'A music that has neither beginning nor end.'" Ned Rorem, review of *Nadia Boulanger: A Life in Music*, by Leonie Rosensteil, *The New York Times Book Review*, 23 May 1982, p. 28.